Collins

INTERNATIONAL PRIMARY MATHS

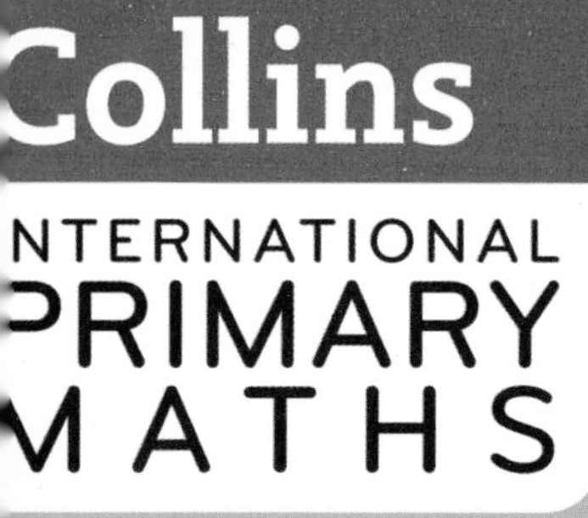

Student's Book 5

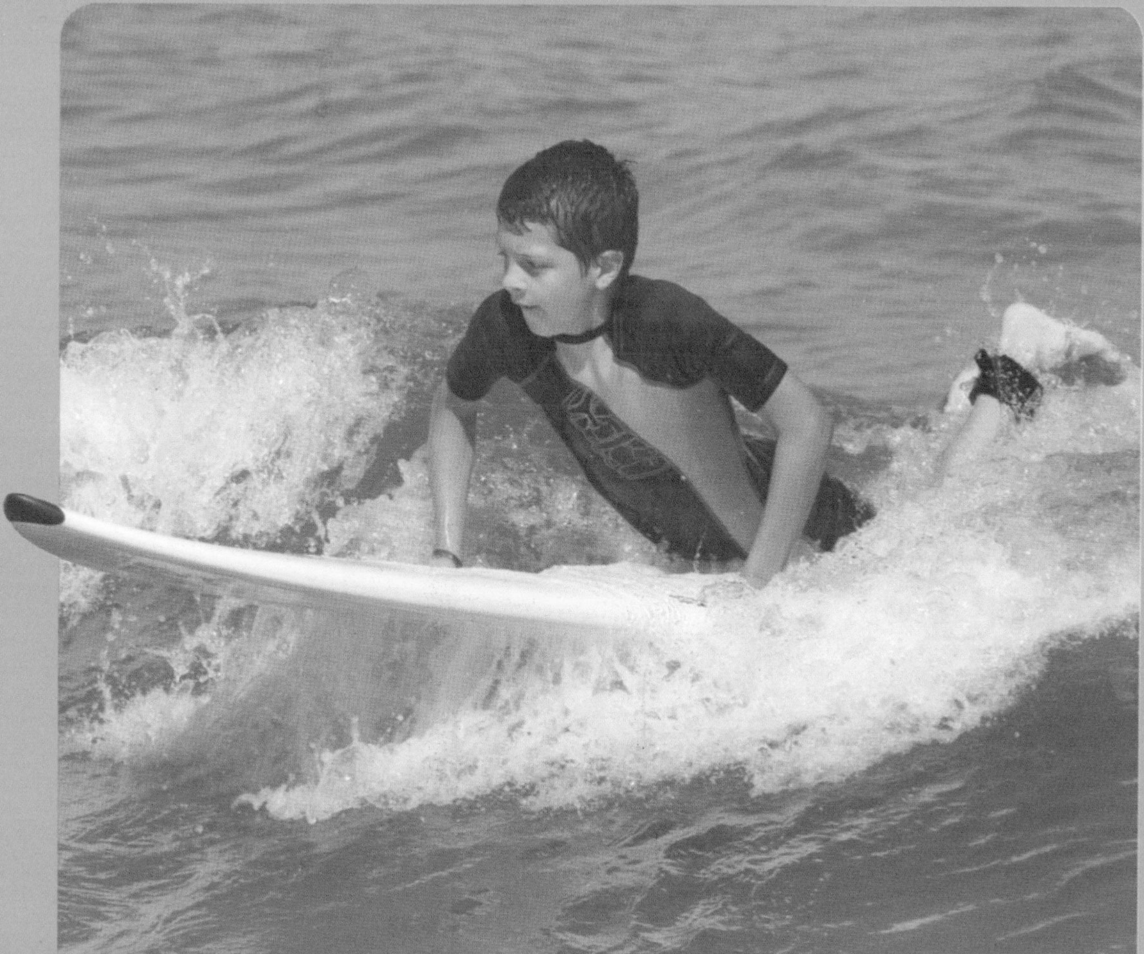

William Collins' dream of knowledge for all began with the publication of his first book in 1819. A self-educated mill worker, he not only enriched millions of lives, but also founded a flourishing publishing house. Today, staying true to this spirit, Collins books are packed with inspiration, innovation and practical expertise. They place you at the centre of a world of possibility and give you exactly what you need to explore it.

Collins. Freedom to teach.

An imprint of HarperCollins*Publishers*
The News Building
1 London Bridge Street
London
SE1 9GF

Browse the complete Collins catalogue at www.collins.co.uk

10 9 8 7 6 5 4 3 2 1

ISBN 978-0-00-815999-3

British Library Cataloguing in Publication Data
A catalogue record for this publication is available from the British Library.

Publishing manager Fiona McGlade
Series editor Peter Clarke
Managing editor Caroline Green
Editor Kate Ellis
Project managed by Emily Hooton
Developed by Joan Miller, Tracy Thomas and Karen Williams
Edited by Tanya Solomons
Proofread by Tracy Thomas
Cover design by Amparo Barrera
Cover artwork by sylv1rob1/Shutterstock
Internal design by Ken Vail Graphic Design Ltd
Typesetting by Ken Vail Graphic Design Ltd
Illustrations by Ken Vail Graphic Design Ltd, Advocate Art and Beehive Illustration
Production by Lauren Crisp

Printed and bound by Grafica Veneta S. P. A.

Contents

Number

Geometry

Measure

Handling data

Lesson 1: **Counting on and back (1)**

- Count on and back in steps of equal size

Key words
- step
- sequence
- count on
- count back

Number

Discover

Counting forwards and backwards in steps helps you understand the pattern and sequence of number.

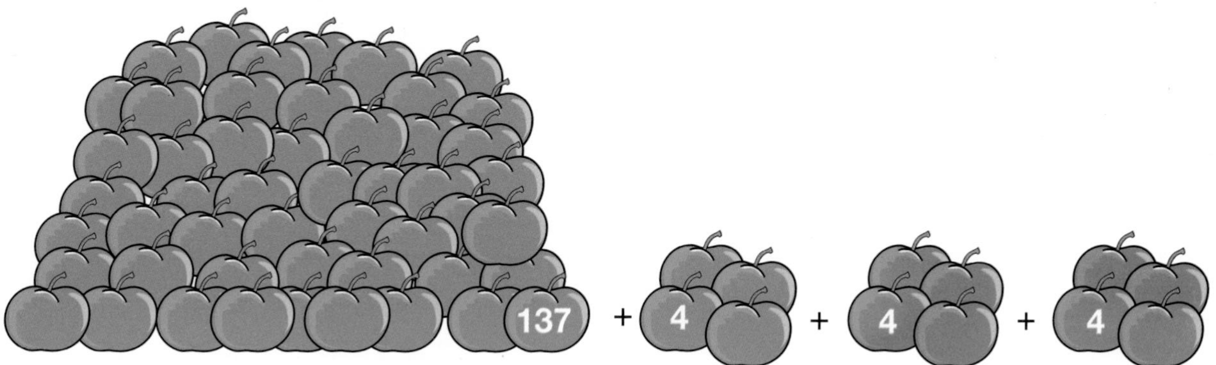

Learn

You can use a number line to explore forwards and backwards counting sequences.

You can start at any point on the line and count on or back in whole numbers or decimals.

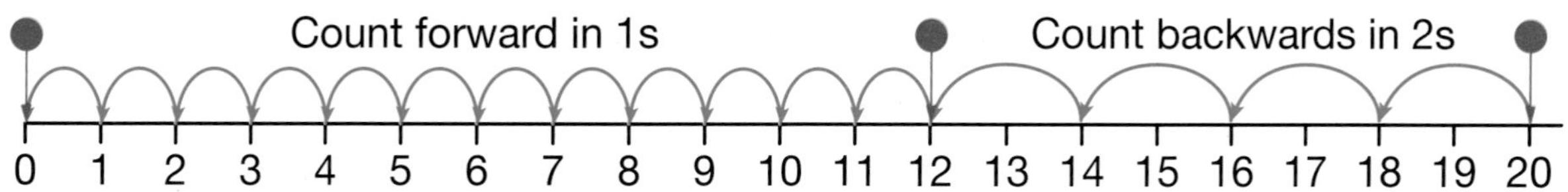

Example

Count back from 43 in steps of 3. Is 28 in this sequence?

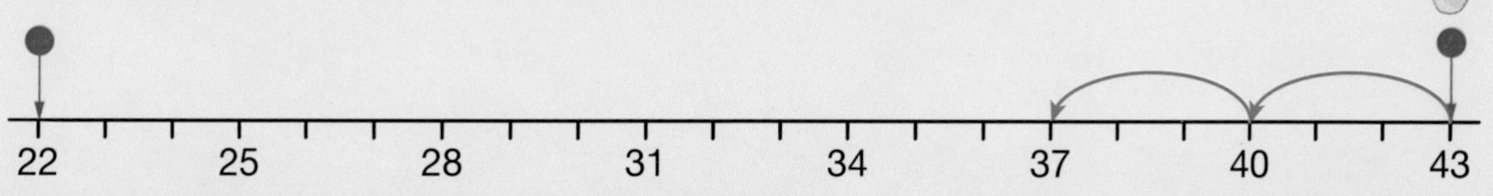

Put your finger on 43 and count back in 3s:

43, 40, 37, 34, 31, 28, 25, 22....yes, 28 is part of this sequence.

Workbook page 4

Lesson 2: **Number sequences**

- Describe number sequences and find the rule

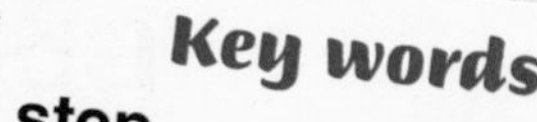

Key words
- step
- rule
- sequence
- value
- term
- common difference

Discover

The black keys on the piano are arranged in a sequence, 3, 2, 3, 2 … .

Learn

A sequence is an ordered list of numbers called **terms**. Each term has a **value**. Every sequence has a **rule**. Once you know the rule, you can work out the next term in the sequence.

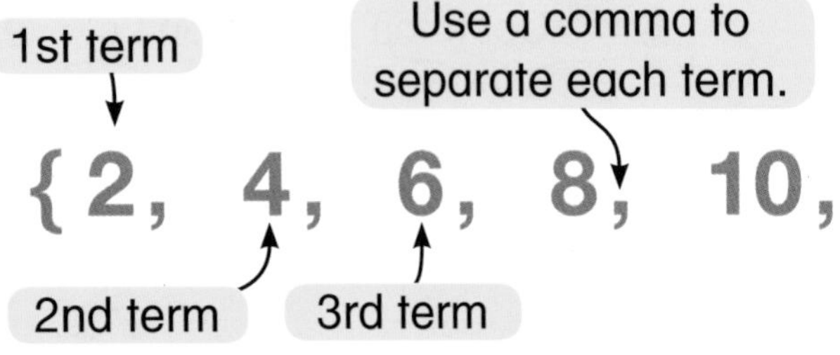

Example

There are eight **terms** in this sequence.

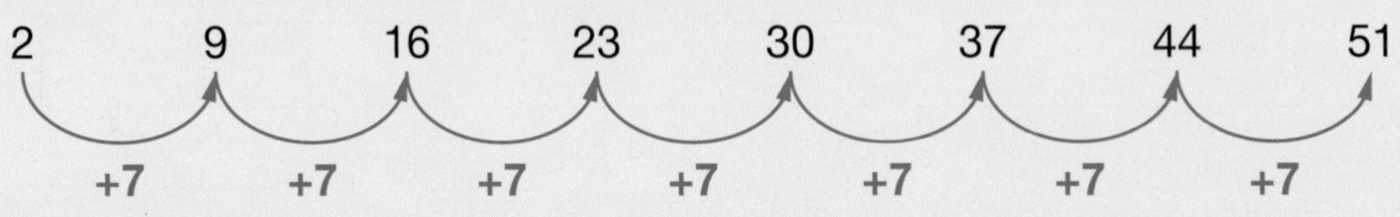

The **values** in the sequence are {2, 9, 16, 23, …} The **rule** is 'add 7'.

Lesson 3: **Place value (1)**

- Know what each digit represents in a five- or six-digit number

Key words
- place value
- digit
- hundred thousands
- ten thousands

Discover

Place value helps you understand the value of a digit in a number.

21 409 g

or

21 940 g

Learn

The value of a digit depends on its place, or position, in the number.

Each place has a value of 10 times the place to its right.

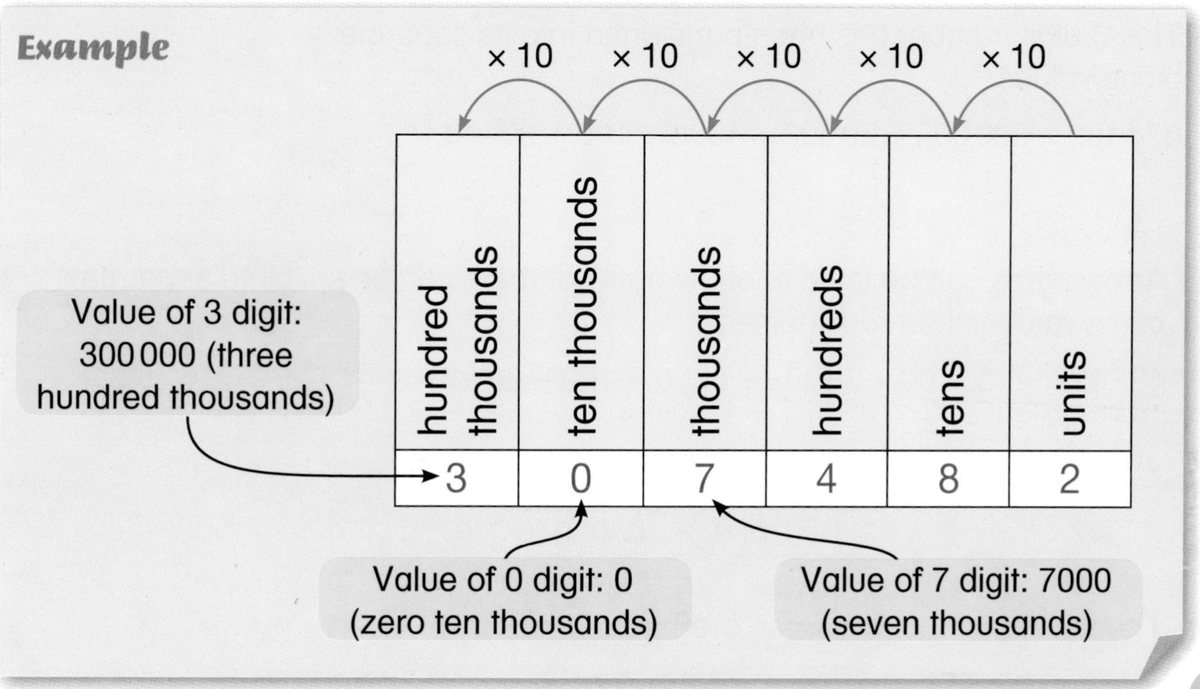

hundred thousands	ten thousands	thousands	hundreds	tens	units
3	0	7	4	8	2

Workbook page 8

Lesson 4: **Place value (2)**

- Use place value to partition any number up to one million

Key words
- place value
- digit
- partition

Discover

Knowing the value of each of the digits in a number is very important, because adding and subtracting often need you to exchange one value for another.

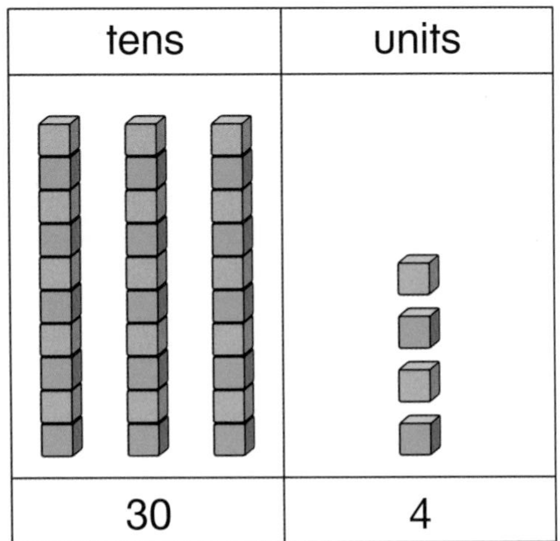

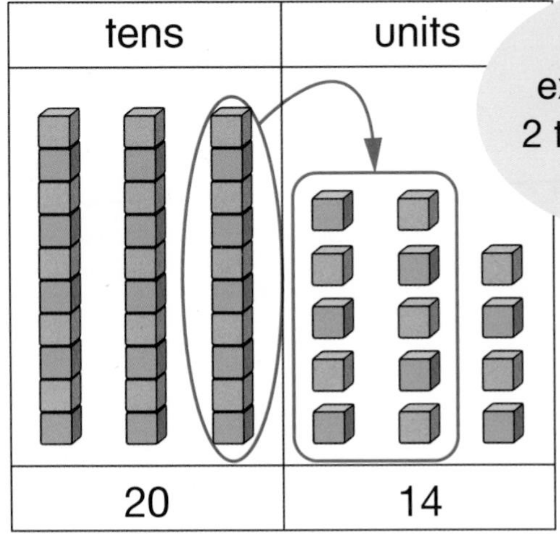

34 can be expressed as 2 tens (20) and 14 units.

Learn

To exchange one value for another it is important to know how to split a number into thousands, hundreds, tens and units.

This 6-digit number has been partitioned into its separate place values.

634 129 = 600 000 + 30 000 + 4000 + 100 + 20 + 9

Example

Arrow cards can be used to show how numbers can be split into separate place values, then recombined.

438 129 = 400 000 + 30 000 + 8000 + 100 + 20 + 9

4 3 8 1 2 9

4 0 0 0 0 0

3 0 0 0 0   8 0 0 0

1 0 0   2 0   9

Number

Lesson 5: Multiplying and dividing by 10 or 100

- Multiply and divide whole numbers by 10 or 100

Key words
- place value
- multiply
- divide

Discover

Multiplying and dividing by 10 or 100 can help you to convert metric measurements and find percentages.

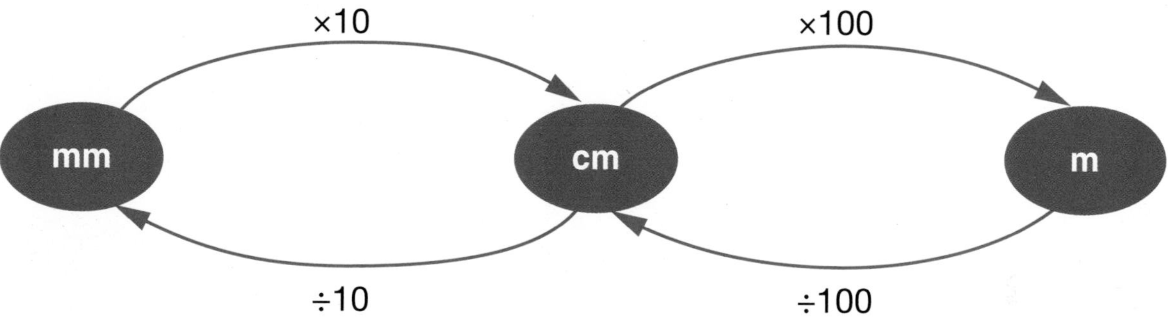

Learn

Multiply by 10: Move all digits one place value to the left.
Multiply by 100: Move all digits two place values to the left.

Example

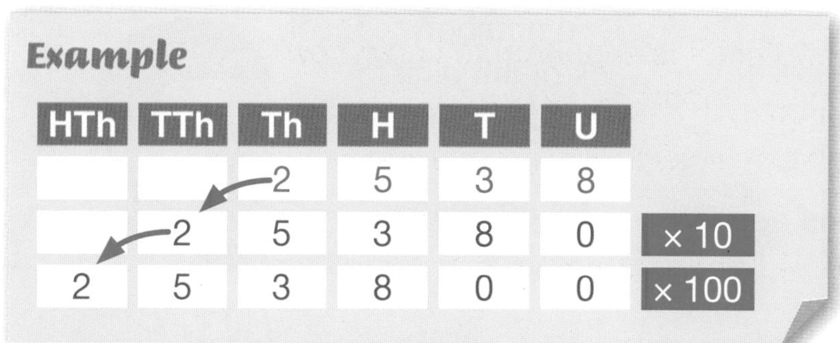

HTh	TTh	Th	H	T	U	
		2	5	3	8	
	2	5	3	8	0	× 10
2	5	3	8	0	0	× 100

Divide by 10: Move all digits one place value to the right.
Divide by 100: Move all digits two place values to the right.

Example

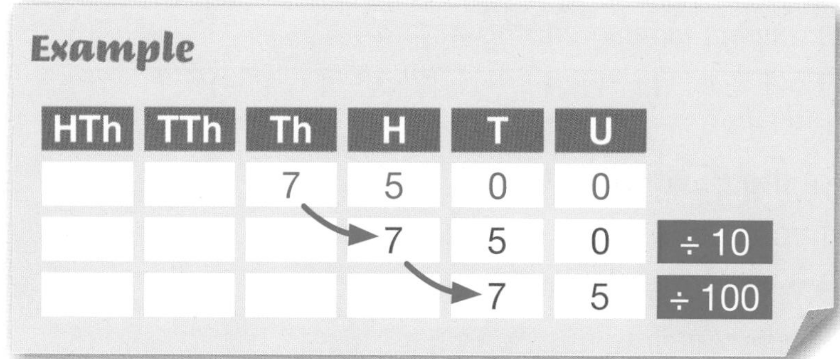

HTh	TTh	Th	H	T	U	
		7	5	0	0	
			7	5	0	÷ 10
				7	5	÷ 100

Workbook page 12

Lesson 6: **Rounding**

- Round 4-digit numbers to the nearest 10, 100 or 1000

Key words
- round
- rounding digit
- nearest 10
- nearest 100
- nearest 1000

Discover

The exact number of fans at a football match was 56 327, but the newspaper says there were 56 330.

They have rounded the number to the nearest 10.

Learn

If the digit is:

- 5 or greater, round up
- less than 5, the whole number remains the same.

Include place holder zeros as needed.

To round a number, look at the digit to the right of the place position you are rounding to.

Example

Round 3862 to the nearest hundred.

3862 is between 3800 and 3900.

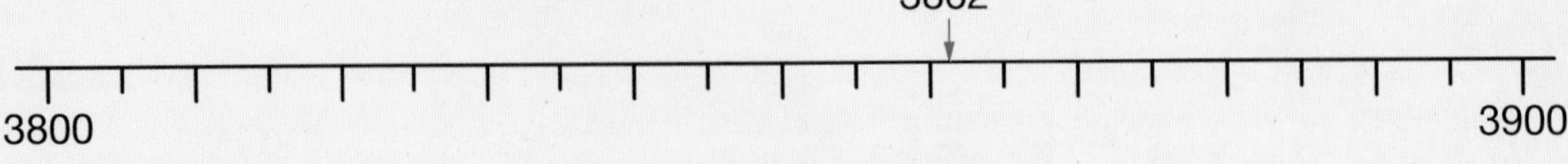

Look at the number to right of the 8, which is 6.

6 is greater than 5, so round up to 3900.

Replace the rest of the digits with placeholder zeros.

Lesson 7: Comparing and ordering

- Use the > and < signs to order and compare numbers up to a million

Key words
- place value
- digit
- thousands
- hundreds
- tens
- units

Number

Discover

Place value can help you to put large numbers in order.

The diameter of Earth, Uranus and Neptune can be put in order by looking at the ten thousands place.

Earth 12 756 km < Neptune 49 528 km < Uranus 51 118 km.

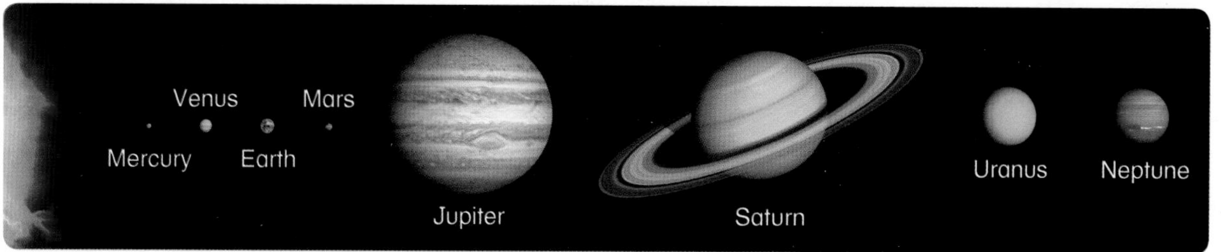

Learn

- Compare digits in each place position, starting on the left.
- If the left-most digit is the same, compare digits in the next place to right.
- When two numbers have different digits in the same place, the number containing the larger digit is the larger number.

We can compare whole numbers with the same number of digits.

Example

HTh	TTh	Th	H	T	U
	4	5	1	3	7
	3	7	8	9	8
	4	7	3	5	2

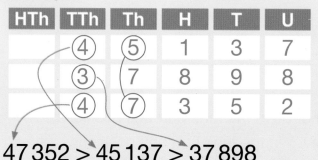

47 352 > 45 137 > 37 898

37 898 is the smallest number; then comparing the next digit (thousand place) 47 352 is the larger number.

Lesson 8: **Odds, evens and multiples (1)**

- Recognise odd and even numbers and multiples of 5, 10, 25, 50 and 100

Key words
- odd
- even
- multiple

Discover

The door numbers on the blue doors are multiples of 25 but not 50.

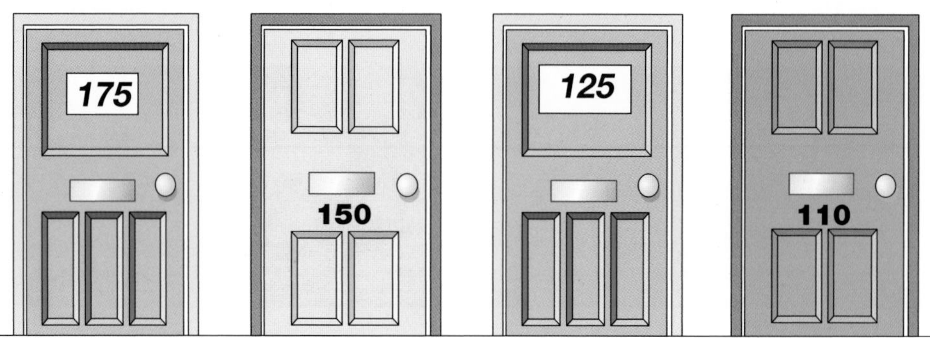

Learn

Numbers with 00, 25, 50 or 75 in the tens and units positions are multiples of 25.

Numbers with 00 or 50 in the tens and units positions are multiples of 50.

Numbers which end in 1, 3, 5, 7 or 9 are odd numbers.

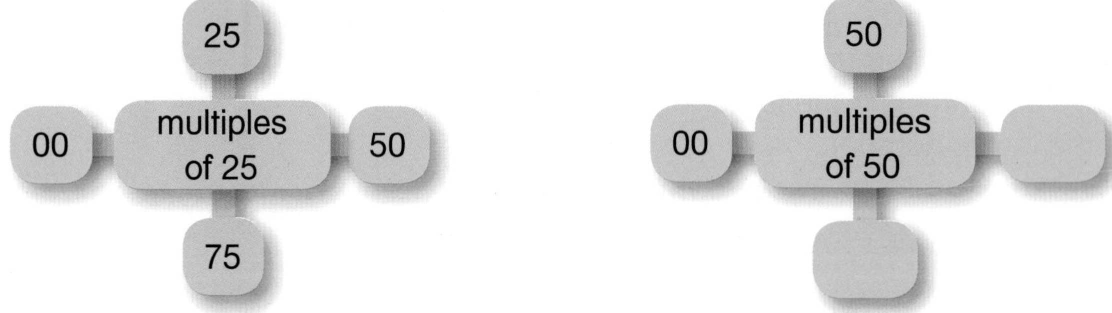

Example

Which of the following numbers are multiples of 25 but not 50: 200, 650, 2275, 4300, 6625?

Multiples of both 25 and 50 have 00 or 50 in the tens and unit positions.

Multiples of 50 but not 25 have 25 or 75 in the tens and unit positions.

So, only 2275 and 6625 are multiples of 25 but not 50.

Lesson 1: **Whole numbers**

- Describe and continue number sequences, including negative numbers

Key words

- **negative number**
- **positive number**
- **step**
- **sequence**
- **count on**
- **count back**

Number

Discover

We use negative numbers to describe a value on a scale that goes below zero.

The temperature on this thermometer reads –5 °C.

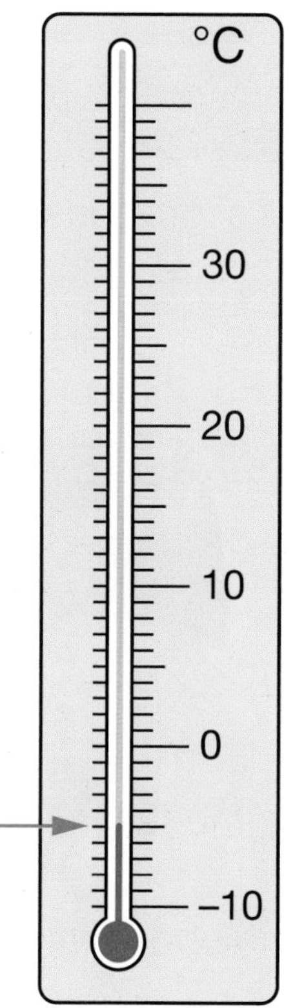

How do temperature and money both use negative numbers?

Learn

Positive numbers are greater than zero.

Negative numbers are less than zero.

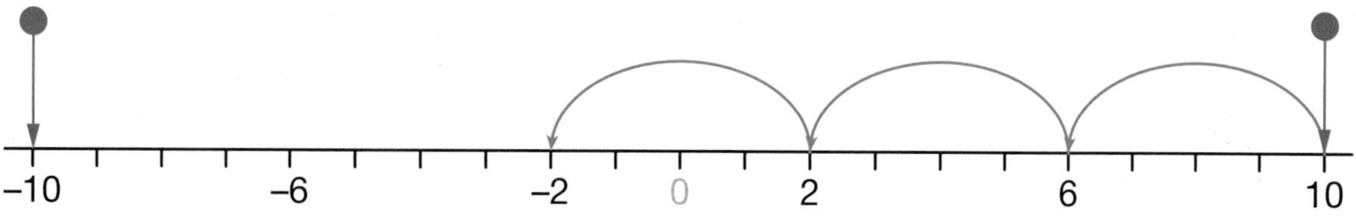

Count back from 10 in steps of 4. Is –4 in this sequence?

Place your finger on 10 and count back in 4s to check.

Workbook page 20

Lesson 2: **Positive and negative numbers**

- Order and compare negative and positive numbers on a number line and temperature scale

Key words
- negative number
- positive number
- order
- thermometer
- temperature
- degrees Celsius (°C)

Discover

In golf, the player with the lowest score wins. Sometimes it can be a negative score.

Position	Name	Score
1st	Jason Day	–5
2nd	Jordan Spieth	–3
3rd	Rory McIlroy	–1
4th	Bubba Watson	2
5th	Louis Oothuizen	4

Learn

Writing numbers on a number line makes it easier to order positive and negative numbers.

Numbers on the left are smaller than numbers on the right.

Numbers on the right are greater than numbers on the left.

Example

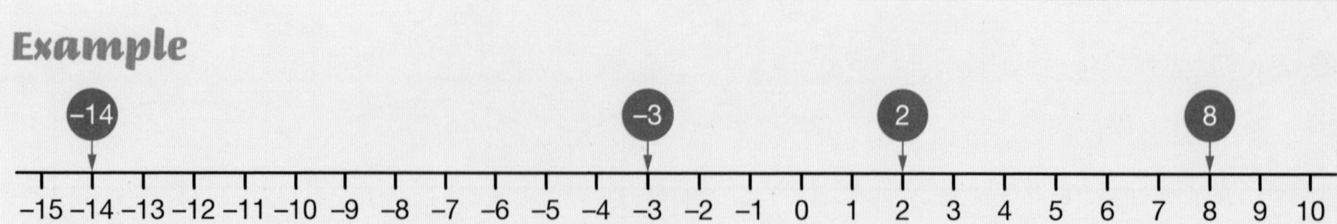

Placing numbers on the number line shows that:

$-14 < -3 < 2 < 8$

Lesson 3: **Calculating temperature change**

- Work out differences between temperature readings on a thermometer

Key words
- negative number
- positive number
- thermometer
- temperature
- degrees Celsius (°C)

Number

Discover

Recording temperatures at different times lets you work out temperature changes.

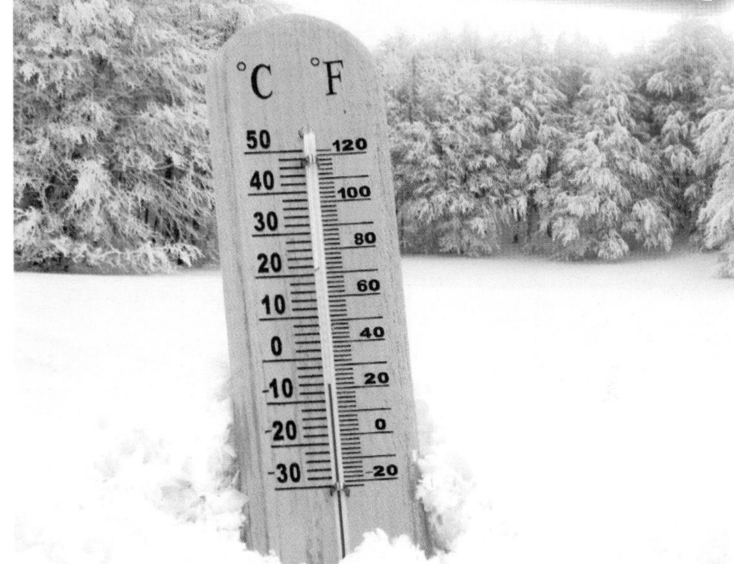

To work out the decrease in temperature:

Learn

1 Work out the difference between the positive value and 0 °C.

2 Work out the difference between 0 °C and the negative value.

3 Add the two numbers together.

Tuesday night: –3 °C

Wednesday afternoon: 8 °C

8 °C to 0 °C is 8 degrees.

–3 °C to 0 °C is 3 degrees.

The temperature change is 8 + 3 = 11 degrees.

By counting from –3 up to 0 and then from 0 to 8 you can see that the temperature has risen by 11 degrees.

Lesson 4: Odds, evens and multiples (2)

- Make general statements about sums, differences and multiples of odd and even numbers

Key words
- odd
- even

Discover

On this number square the odd numbers are white and the even numbers are blue.

What happens when you add odd and even numbers?

1	2	3	4	5	6	7	8	9	10
11	12	13	14	15	16	17	18	19	20
21	22	23	24	25	26	27	28	29	30
31	32	33	34	35	36	37	38	39	40
41	42	43	44	45	46	47	48	49	50
51	52	53	54	55	56	57	58	59	60
61	62	63	64	65	66	67	68	69	70
71	72	73	74	75	76	77	78	79	80
81	82	83	84	85	86	87	88	89	90
91	92	93	94	95	96	97	98	99	100

Learn

Addition

Even + Even = Even	$4 + 6 = 10$	(even)
Even + Odd = Odd	$6 + 5 = 11$	(odd)
Odd + Even = Odd	$7 + 8 = 15$	(odd)
Odd + Odd = Even	$5 + 3 = 8$	(even)

Subtraction

Even – Even = Even	$12 - 4 = 8$	(even)
Even – Odd = Odd	$8 - 3 = 5$	(odd)
Odd – Even = Odd	$9 - 2 = 7$	(odd)
Odd – Odd = Even	$9 - 5 = 4$	(even)

Multiplication

Even × Even = Even	$4 \times 6 = 24$	(even)
Even × Odd = Even	$8 \times 3 = 24$	(even)
Odd × Even = Even	$5 \times 6 = 30$	(even)
Odd × Odd = Odd	$7 \times 9 = 63$	(odd)

Lesson 1: **Tenths**

- Write tenths in decimals and understand what each digit represents
- Count up and down in tenths

Key words
- fraction
- decimal fraction
- tenths

Discover

People use decimals every day, particularly in calculations involving measurements. For example, when a weighing scale reads 5·3 kg you need to know that the digit to the right of the decimal point is in the tenths position and represents 0·3 kg or 3 tenths of a kilogram.

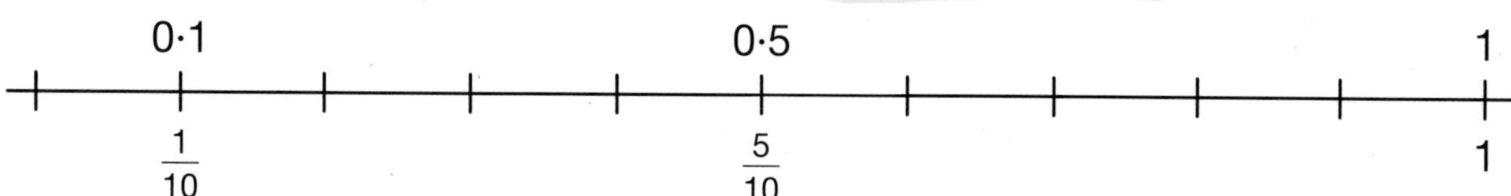

Learn

The number line between 0 and 1 can be divided into 10 parts.

Each of these 10 parts is $\frac{1}{10}$, a tenth.

You can write any fraction in tenths as a decimal.

After the decimal point, write how many tenths the number has.

Example

Write the shaded amount as a fraction and as a decimal.

$\frac{3}{10}$ or 0·3

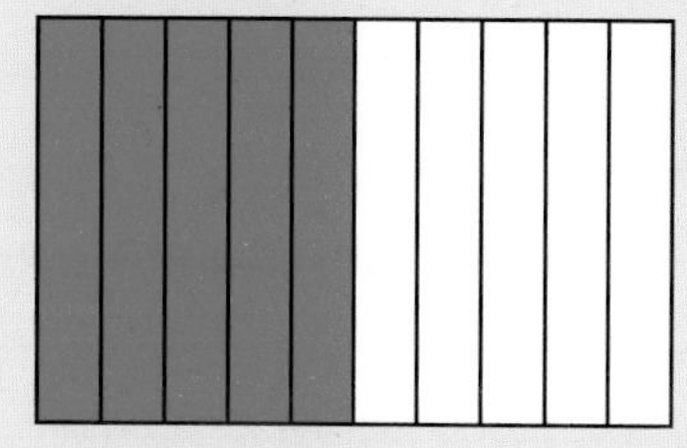

$\frac{5}{10}$ or 0·5

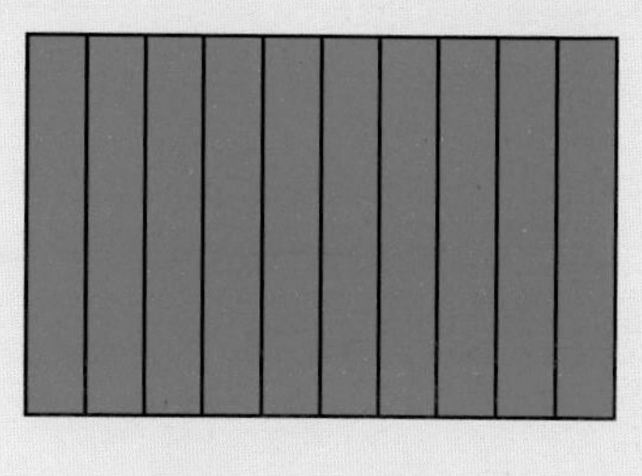

$\frac{10}{10}$ or 1·0

Lesson 2: **Hundredths**

- Recognise that hundredths arise when dividing an object by 100
- Recognise and write decimal equivalents of any number of hundredths

Key words
- fraction
- decimal fraction
- hundredths
- denominator

Number

Discover

A dollar is divided into 100 parts, each called a 'cent'. One cent is one hundredth of a dollar and is written 1c or \$0.01.

Learn

On a number line, we get hundredths by dividing each interval of one tenth into 10 new parts.

0.3 0.4

As a decimal, one hundredth is written 0·01 and as a fraction it is written $\frac{1}{100}$.
It is the second digit after the decimal point.

Example

Write the shaded amount as a fraction and as a decimal.

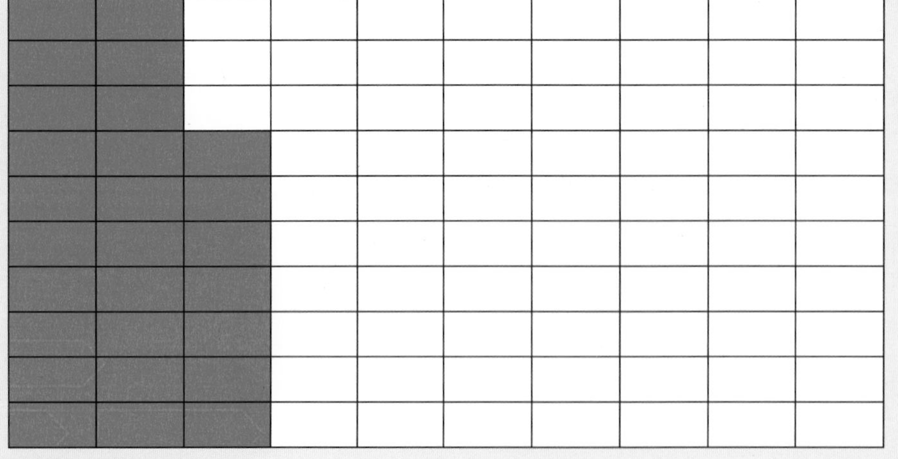

$\frac{27}{100} = 0{\cdot}27$

Lesson 3: **Multiplying by 10 or 100**

- Multiply any number by 10 or 100.

Key words
- units
- tenths
- hundredths
- multiply
- place value

Discover

If one book costs $11, is this offer really a bargain?

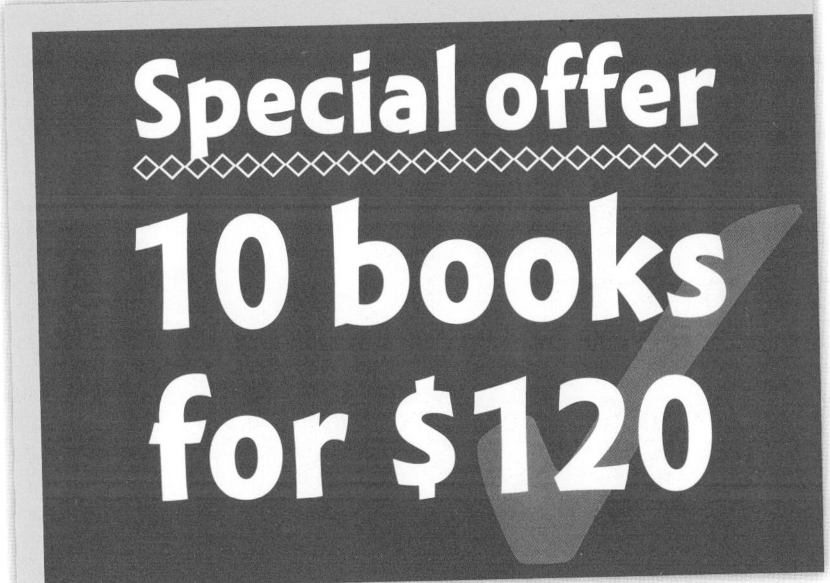

Learn

When multiplied by 10, a number becomes 10 times larger and the digits move 1 place to the left.

When multiplied by 100, a number becomes 100 times larger and the digits move 2 places to the left.

Example

245 × 10 = 2450	7083 × 10 = 70 830
245 × 100 = 24 500	7083 × 100 = 708 300

Workbook page 32

Lesson 4: **Dividing by 10 or 100**

- Divide any number by 10 or 100.

Key words
- units
- tenths
- hundredths
- divide
- place value

Discover

If one bar is priced at $0.86, is this offer really a bargain?

Special offer
100 chocolate bars for $85!
$0·86

Learn

When divided by 10, a number becomes 10 times smaller and the digits move 1 place to the right. A digit in the units column will move across the decimal point to the tenths column.

When divided by 100, a number becomes 100 times smaller and the digits move 2 places to the right. A digit in the tens column will move across the decimal point to the tenths column and a digit in the units column will move across to the hundredths column.

Example

24 ÷ 10 = 2·4	24 ÷ 100 = 0·24
246 ÷ 10 = 24·6	246 ÷ 100 = 2·46

Lesson 1: Tenths and hundredths

- Use decimal notation for tenths and hundredths
- Write decimals in expanded form

Key words
- decimal fraction
- tenth
- hundredth
- place value
- expanded form

Discover

How would you pay for an item that is priced $4.16 in a shop?

Think of the price as a decimal number. Does this help you decide which notes and coins you would use to pay?

Learn

Each position in a decimal number corresponds to a power of 10. In the number 0·33 the 3 in the tenths position is 10 times bigger than the 3 in the hundredths position.

A decimal number can be split into its separate place values. This is sometimes called the expanded form.

Example

0·46 = 0·4 + 0·06 0·75 = 0·7 + 0·05

Number

Lesson 2: **Comparing decimals**

- Compare numbers with 1 or 2 decimal places

Key words
- decimal
- decimal place
- place value

Discover

If you were asked to compare the heights of two trees, 18·43 m and 18·47 m, you would know by place value that the tree 18·47 m high was taller: 18·47 > 18·43.

Learn

Write the numbers to be compared in a place value grid, with the decimal points lined up.

Start by comparing whole numbers, then the values of the digits in the tenths place. If the digits are the same, move to the hundredths place and compare values.

For each position, a digit of greater value indicates the larger number.

Example

Which is larger, 2·21 or 2·12?

2·21 > 2·12

tens	units		tenths	hundredths
	2	·	2	1
	2	·	1	2

Lesson 3: **Ordering decimals**

- Order numbers with 1 or 2 decimal places

Key words
- decimal
- decimal place
- place value

Discover

100 m runners often record times in fractions of seconds, such as 11·82s.

Being able to order decimal numbers is important, particularly when it concerns race finishing times.

A: 12·63s	B: 12·03s	C: 12·61s	D: 12·07s	E: 12·36s

Learn

To order a set of decimals from largest to smallest by place value:

1 Organise the numbers with the decimal points lined up.
2 Compare the digits in columns from left to right.
3 If the digits are the same, move to the next column until a digit is larger.
4 This is the largest number in the set.
5 Repeat steps 2 and 3 until all the numbers are in order, largest to smallest.

Example

Order the numbers 3·45, 3·25, 3·42, 3·07 and 3·27 from smallest to largest.

3·45 Largest number; larger than 3·42 as 5 hundredths > 2 hundredths
3·25 4th largest
3·42 2nd largest
3·07 Smallest number
3·27 3rd largest; larger than 3·25 as 7 hundredths > 5 hundredths

3·07, 3·25, 3·27, 3·42, 3·45

Lesson 4: **Rounding decimals**

- Round any number with 1 or 2 decimal places to the nearest whole number

Key words
- round
- decimal
- 1 decimal place
- 2 decimal places
- hundredths
- tenths

Discover

Laila has chosen four items she'd like to buy when she has saved enough money.

The prices are \$6.95, \$8.02, \$3.98 and \$5.01. Laila remembers them as \$7, \$8, \$4 and \$5.

What has Laila done and how does this help her?

Learn

To round decimals to the nearest whole number, look at the digit in the tenths position.

- 5 or greater: round up to the next whole number.
- Less than 5: the whole number remains the same.

Example

Round 11·17, 7·51 and 27·83 to the nearest whole number.

11·17 is 11 as the tenths digit is less than 5.

7·51 is 8 as the tenths digit is 5.

27·83 is 28 as the tenths digit is greater than 5.

Lesson 1: Equivalent fractions

- Identify, name and write equivalent fractions of a given fraction

Key words
- equivalent
- numerator
- denominator
- like fraction
- unlike fraction

Number

Discover

50 cents is half of a dollar, just as 50 cents is half of 100 cents $\left(\frac{50}{100}\right)$: $\frac{1}{2} = \frac{50}{100}$.

Learn

Equivalent fractions have different names, but have the same value. They are in the same place on a number line.

$\frac{1}{2} = \frac{2}{4} = \frac{4}{8} = \frac{5}{10}$ $\frac{1}{3} = \frac{2}{6}$ $\frac{1}{5} = \frac{2}{10}$

Example

Use a diagram, such as a fraction wall, to identify equivalent fractions.

$\frac{1}{2}$, $\frac{2}{4}$ and $\frac{4}{8}$ are all equivalent fractions.

They take up the same length on the fraction wall.

<table>
<tr><td colspan="8">1</td></tr>
<tr><td colspan="4">$\frac{1}{2}$</td><td colspan="4">$\frac{1}{2}$</td></tr>
<tr><td colspan="2">$\frac{1}{4}$</td><td colspan="2">$\frac{1}{4}$</td><td colspan="2">$\frac{1}{4}$</td><td colspan="2">$\frac{1}{4}$</td></tr>
<tr><td>$\frac{1}{8}$</td><td>$\frac{1}{8}$</td><td>$\frac{1}{8}$</td><td>$\frac{1}{8}$</td><td>$\frac{1}{8}$</td><td>$\frac{1}{8}$</td><td>$\frac{1}{8}$</td><td>$\frac{1}{8}$</td></tr>
</table>

Workbook page 44

Lesson 2: **Fraction and decimal equivalents**

Key words

- equivalent
- mixed number
- fraction
- decimal
- tenths
- hundredths

- Recognise fractions and decimals that are equivalent and use this to help order fractions

Discover

It can be useful to be able to convert one kind of number into another.

For example, it is easier to add the measures $\frac{1}{10}$ litre and 0·5 litre if you convert $\frac{1}{10}$ into a decimal.

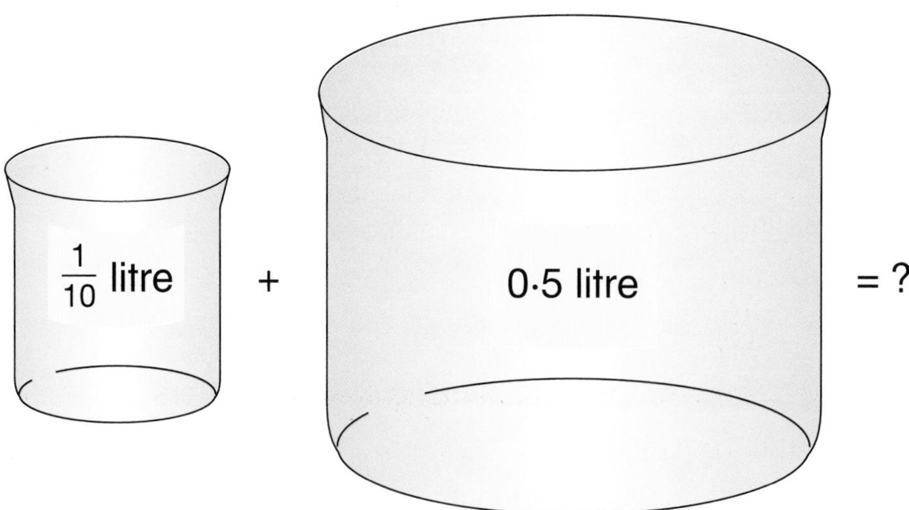

Learn

0·5 is equivalent to $\frac{5}{10}$ or $\frac{1}{2}$

0·1 is equivalent to $\frac{1}{10}$

0·25 is equivalent to $\frac{25}{100}$ or $\frac{1}{4}$

0·75 is equivalent to $\frac{75}{100}$ or $\frac{3}{4}$

Example

$\frac{2}{4}$ + 0·25

Convert 0·25 to $\frac{1}{4}$.

$\frac{2}{4} + \frac{1}{4} = \frac{3}{4}$

0·25

$\frac{1}{2}$

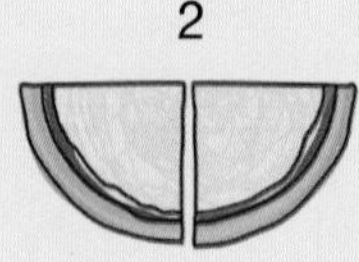

$\frac{3}{4}$

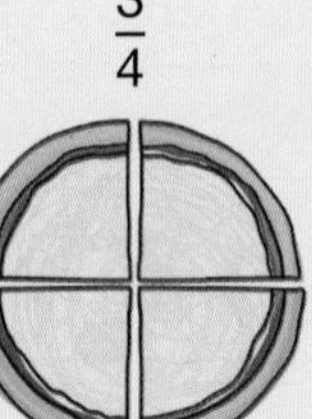

Lesson 3: **Mixed numbers**

- Convert improper fractions to mixed numbers
- Order a set of mixed numbers

Key words
- numerator
- denominator
- improper fraction
- proper fraction
- mixed number

Discover

In an improper fraction, the numerator (top number) is greater than, or equal to, the denominator (bottom number).

In mathematics, improper fractions are often easier to use than mixed numbers, but most people prefer mixed numbers as they are easier to read. Therefore it's important to be able to convert improper fractions to mixed numbers.

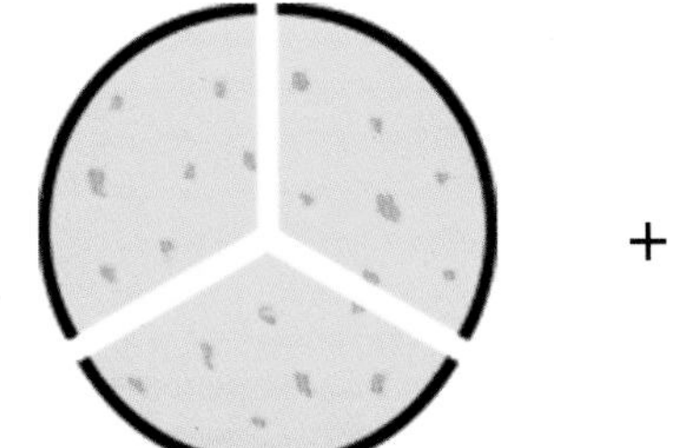 + 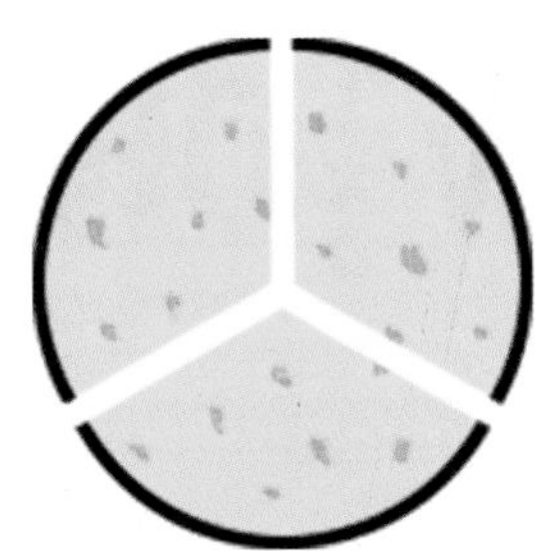 + 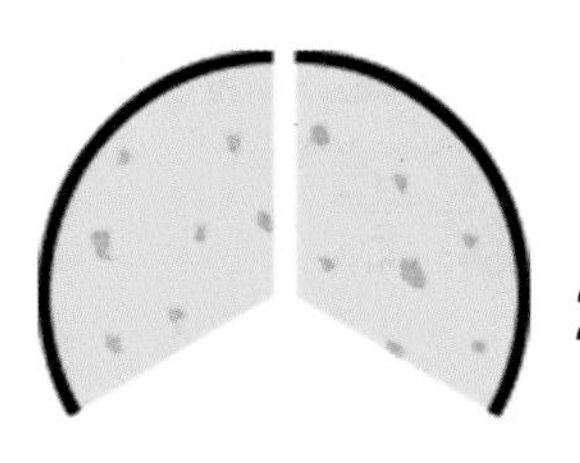 $2\frac{2}{3}$

Learn

A visual model can help convert improper fractions to mixed numbers.

Here is a circle model for the fraction $\frac{13}{3}$.

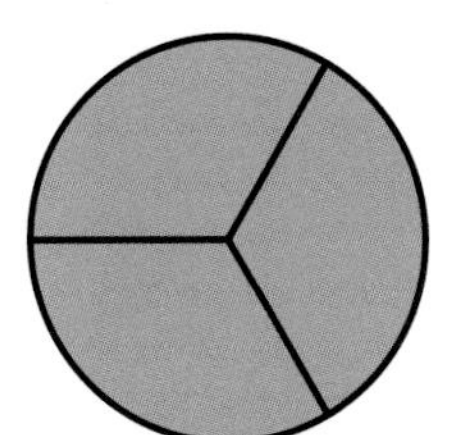 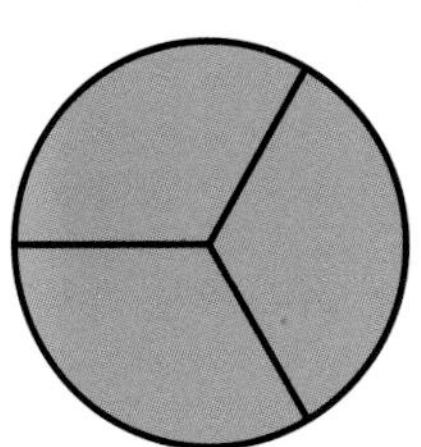 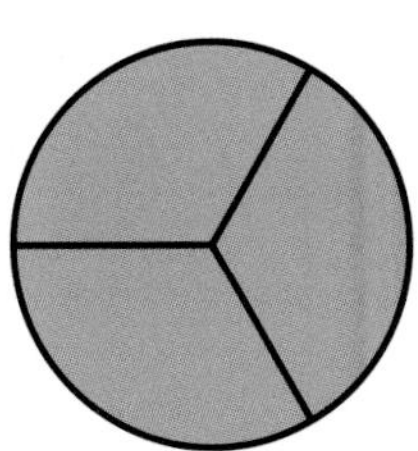 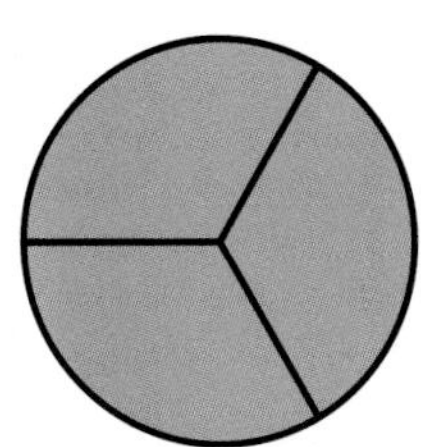 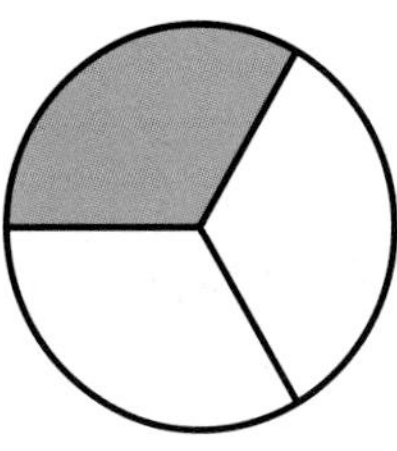

Think visually!

$$\frac{13}{3} = \frac{3}{3} + \frac{3}{3} + \frac{3}{3} + \frac{3}{3} + \frac{1}{3} = 4\frac{1}{3}$$

Example

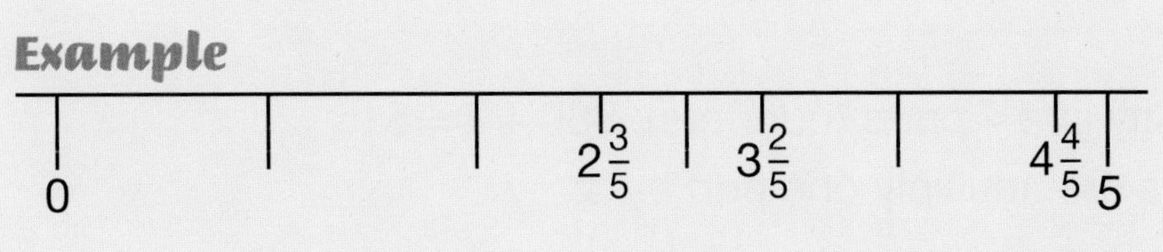

Lesson 4: Fractions of quantities

- Find simple fractions of quantities

Key words
- numerator
- denominator
- unit fraction
- non-unit fraction

Discover

Knowing how to find a fraction of a number is a useful skill for reducing recipes or calculating discounts.
If someone went shopping for a new digital camera and saw these two offers, which one should they buy?

Learn

To find the fraction of a quantity:

1. To find one part: divide the quantity by the denominator.
2. To find the required number of parts: multiply the answer to Step 1 by the numerator.

Example

Find $\frac{3}{4}$ of $60.
Divide the whole quantity into 4 parts (quarters): $60 ÷ 4 = $15
To find out what 3 parts are: multiply one part by 3:
$15 × 3 = $45

Lesson 1: Per cent symbol

- Understand percentage as 'the number of parts in every hundred'

Key words
- per cent
- percentage
- hundredths

Discover

100 children stand in 10 rows of 10. One child is wearing a hat. How can you describe how many children are wearing a hat?

You could say one hundredth ($\frac{1}{100}$) are wearing a hat. This can also be expressed as a percentage: 1 per cent or 1%.

Percentages tell us the number of parts in every hundred.

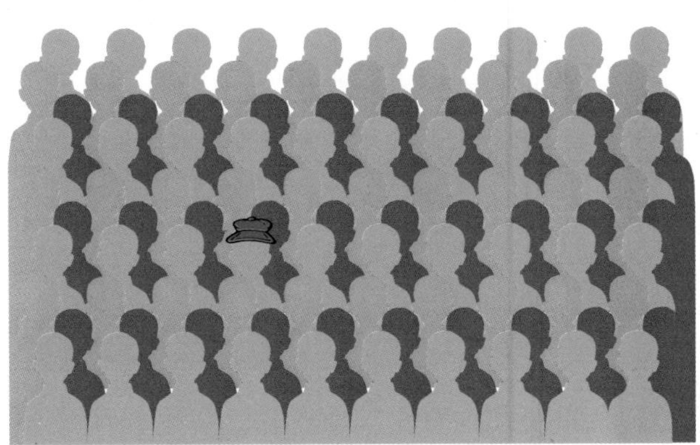

Learn

Per cent means 'for every hundred'. The sign for per cent is %.

If you are thinking of 3 children out of every 100, then you write 3%; and for 17 children you write 17%.

Example

You can use a 100 grid to model percentages.

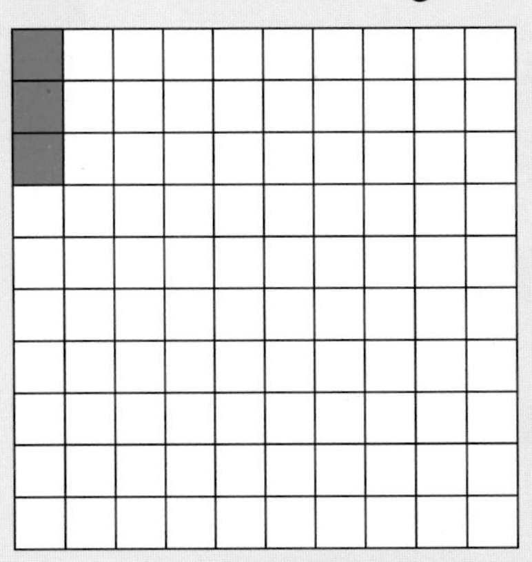

3%

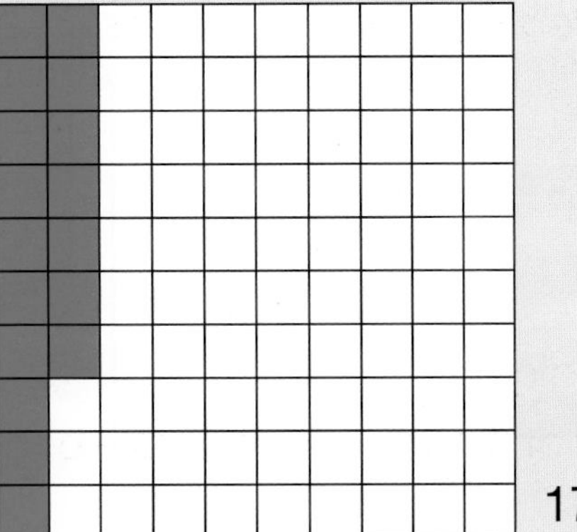

17%

Workbook page 52

Number

Lesson 2: Expressing fractions as percentages

- Write percentages as a fraction with a denominator of 100
- Know percentage equivalents of certain fractions

Key words
- per cent
- percentage
- hundredths
- tenths
- whole
- half
- equivalent

Discover

A gardener says, 'I would like half my flowers to be red and half my flowers to be yellow.' How could you express this using percentages?

Learn

A percentage can be thought of as another name for hundredths.

A fraction expressed as a hundredth can simply be renamed as a percentage.

For example: $\frac{1}{100} = 1\%$ $\frac{27}{100} = 27\%$

Example

$\frac{6}{10}$ of these pencils are blue. This is the same as $\frac{60}{100}$.
So, we can say that 60% of these pencils are blue.

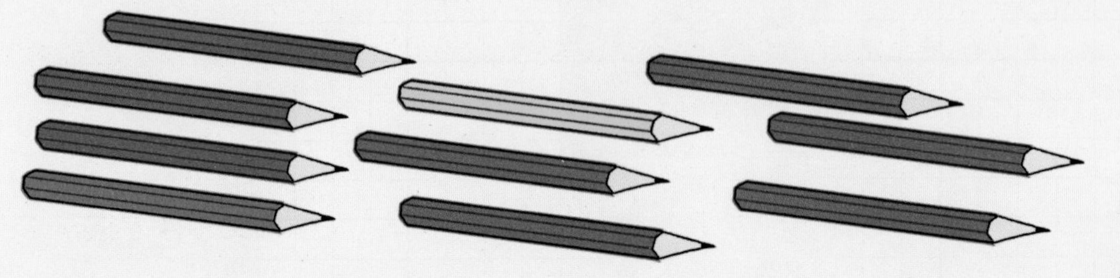

Lesson 3: **Percentages of quantities**

- Find simple percentages of quantities

Key words
- fraction
- per cent
- divide
- multiply

Discover

It is useful to be able to find a percentage of a quantity. For example, a teacher says that 10% of the children in Class 5 have blonde hair. If there are 30 children in the class, then 3 will have blonde hair.

Learn

You can calculate a percentage of an amount by using percentage and fraction equivalents.

$1\% = \frac{1}{100}$ $10\% = \frac{1}{10}$ $25\% = \frac{1}{4}$ $50\% = \frac{1}{2}$

Example

1 What is 10% of $260?

$10\% = \frac{1}{10}$

$\frac{1}{10}$ of \$260

$= \$260 \div 10 = \$26$

2 What is 50% of $260?

$50\% = \frac{1}{2}$

$\frac{1}{2}$ of \$260

$= \$260 \div 2 = \$130$

3 What is 25% of $260?

$25\% = \frac{1}{4}$

$\frac{1}{4}$ of \$260

$= \$260 \div 4 = \$65$

Number

Lesson 4: **Percentage problems**

- Find simple percentages of quantities

Key words
- fraction
- percent
- divide
- multiply

Discover

Problems that involve finding percentages can be quite easy to solve once you have found the right strategy.

In most cases, you just use the relationship between percentages and fractions.

Common fractions and percentages

Fraction	Percentage
$\frac{1}{10}$	10%
$\frac{1}{4}$	25%
$\frac{1}{2}$	50%

Learn

Look at these two ways you can calculate the percentage of an amount.

a) Use percentage and fraction equivalents, for example $25\% = \frac{1}{4}$.

b) Find 1% by dividing by 100. Multiply 1% of the amount to find the percentage you need.

Example

1 What is 25% of \$1200?

$25\% = \frac{1}{4}$

$\frac{1}{4}$ of \$1200 = \$1200 ÷ 4 = \$300

2 What is 75% of \$1200?

25% = \$300

As 75% is 3 × 25% then 75% of \$1200 = 3 × \$300
= \$900

Lesson 1: **Proportion**

- Use fractions to describe and estimate a simple proportion

Key words
- proportion
- in every
- whole
- fraction

Discover

Proportion compares parts to a whole. It is important for keeping things in balance.

In the picture, two of the six flowers are red. Another way to describe this is $\frac{1}{3}$ of the flowers are red.

Learn

Proportion can be described using fractions. Each small box of chocolates contains 1 white chocolate and 3 dark chocolates.

Proportion of white: 1 in every 4. $\frac{1}{4}$ are white.

Proportion of dark: 3 in every 4. $\frac{3}{4}$ are dark.

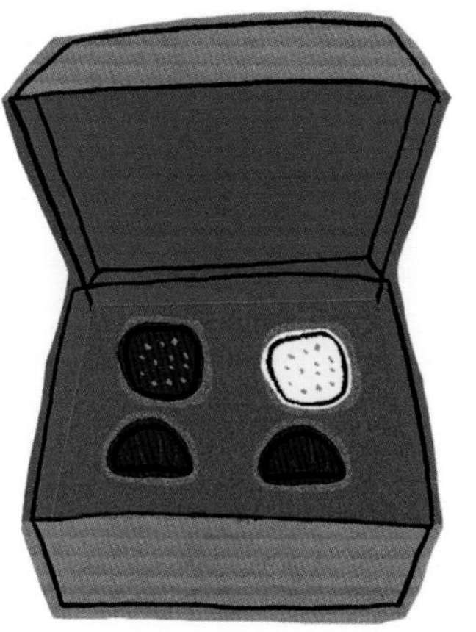

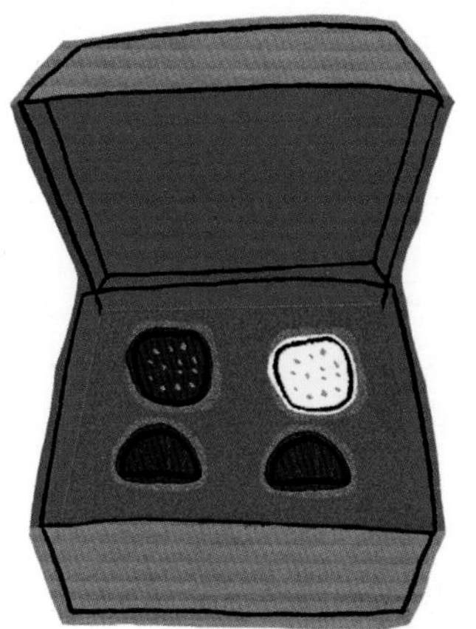

Workbook page 60

Lesson 2: **Proportion problems**

- Solve simple proportion problems

Key words
- proportion
- in every
- whole
- fraction

Discover

Proportion problems give you the value of two or more related items, or parts of a whole, and ask you to work out new values when the size of the whole changes.

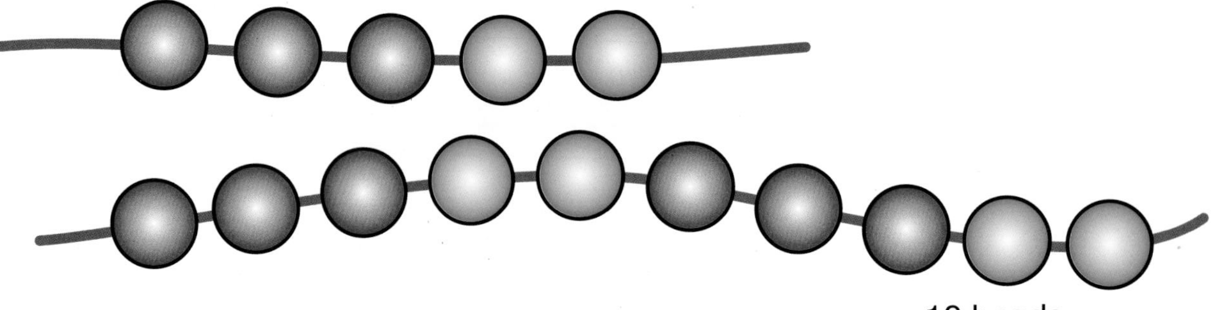

Learn

If you know the number of parts in a whole then you can write the number of parts if the whole number changes. If 2 beads in every 5 beads are blue, then the number of blue beads in 10 beads will be 4 and the number of blue beads in 15 beads will be 6.

Example

The number of beads above increases to 20. How many red beads and blue beads will there be?

The fractions are:

red = $\frac{3}{5}$

blue = $\frac{2}{5}$

The proportion of red to blue is the same for larger necklaces.

Therefore, for 20 beads:

red = $\frac{3}{5}$ of 20 = 12

blue = $\frac{2}{5}$ of 20 = 8

Lesson 3: **Ratio**

- Express parts of a whole as a ratio

Key words
- ratio
- for every
- simplify
- scale factor

Number

Discover

The ratio of red to blue cubes in the pattern shown is 4 red to 2 blue. In other words, there are 4 red cubes for every 2 blue cubes.

Learn and Example

The cubes in the picture above are in the ratio 4 red to 2 blue.

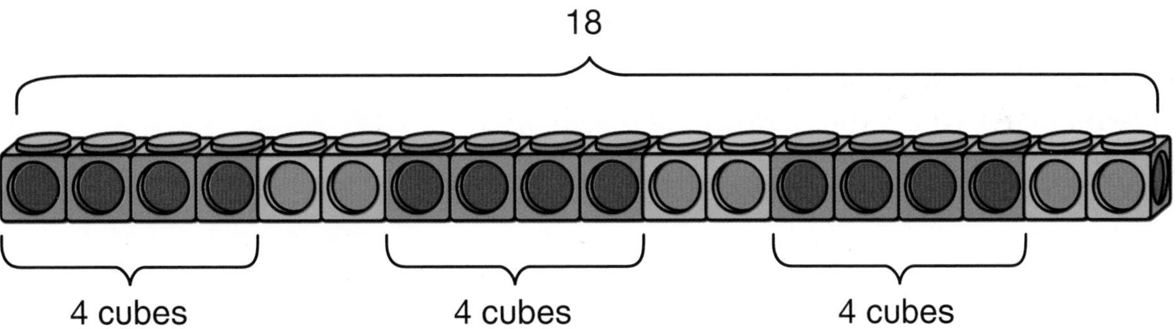

How many red cubes would we need for a pattern built using this ratio that had a total of 18 cubes?

To work this out, we could scale up.

We know there are 3 lots of 6 in 18.

So we would need $3 \times 4 = 12$ red cubes and $3 \times 2 = 6$ blue cubes.

Workbook page 64

Lesson 4: **Ratio problems**

- Solve simple ratio problems

Key words
- ratio
- for every
- simplify
- scale factor

Discover

Ratios can be used to solve many different problems – for example, with recipes. To change the number of servings you want you can scale a recipe up or down.

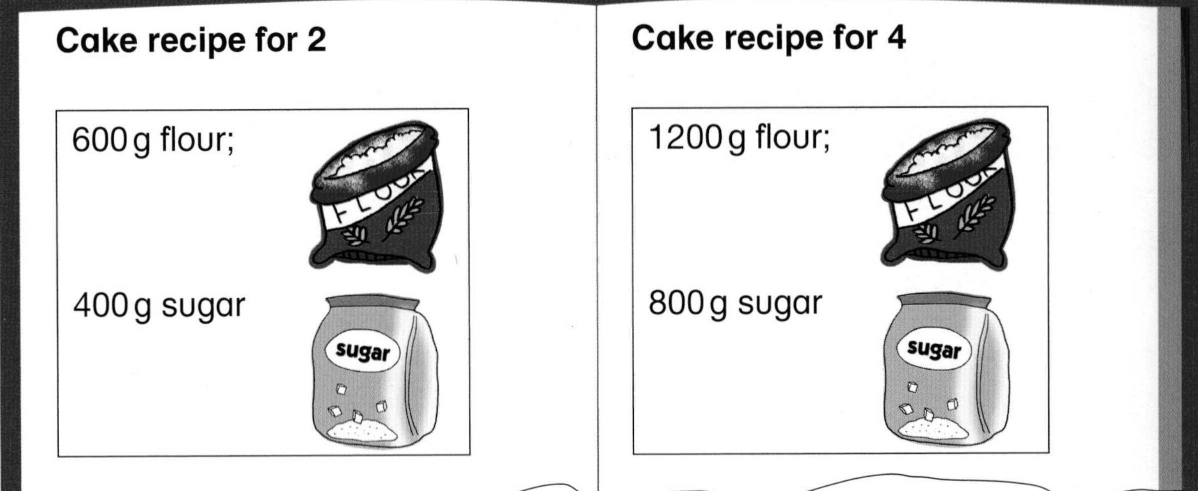

Learn

Ratios can be scaled up or down by multiplying or dividing the values in the ratio.

Cake recipe			
Ingredient	**for 4 people**	**for 8 people**	**for 2 People**
eggs	12	24	6
flour (cups)	8	16	4
sugar (cups)	4	8	2

Example

The ratio for 4 people is 12 eggs, 8 cups of flour and 4 cups of sugar. What are the ingredients for 12 people?

The amount of ingredients for 12 people would be three times that for 4 people.

That is 36 eggs, 24 cups of flour and 12 cups of sugar.

Lesson 1: Counting on or back (2)

Key words
- addition
- units
- tens
- hundreds
- thousands
- multiples of
- tens/hundreds/ thousands boundary

- Count on or back in thousands, hundreds, tens and units to add or subtract

Number

Discover

Learning how to count on or back in tens, hundreds, thousands and beyond helps you understand which digits change and when. It also helps you become faster at adding and subtracting numbers in your head.

You want to buy a TV for $638. You have saved up $237 and you are due to receive four payments of $100 each. Will you have enough to buy the TV?

Balance	PAID IN ON 15/10	$237.00

+

$400.00

Is it enough?

Learn

	Which digits change?				
	units	**tens**	**hundreds**	**thousands**	**ten thousands**
counting in tens	never	each count	next count after tens digit reaches 9	next count after tens and hundreds digits reach 9	next count after tens, hundreds and thousands digits reach 9
counting in hundreds	never	never	each count	next count after hundreds digit reaches 9	next count after hundreds and thousands digits reach 9

Example

4374 + 10 = 4384 4374 + 100 = 4474 4374 + 1000 = 5374

Lesson 2: **Adding 2- and 3-digit numbers**

- Select and use effective strategies to add pairs of 2- and 3-digit numbers

Key words
- addition
- counting on
- partitioning
- bridging
- compensation
- compatible numbers

Discover

68 + 79 = ?

There are many different ways of solving mental addition problems. No one strategy is "right" for every problem. Use a method you feel confident with, which solves the problem as efficiently as possible.

Learn and Example

Some mental strategies for addition

Name	Example
Counting on	Calculate 86 + 30 Count on in 10s, i.e. 96, 106, 116
Partioning	Calculate 237 + 324 Split 237: 200, 30 and 7 / Split 324: 300, 20 and 4 Add hundreds: 200 + 300 = 500 Add tens: 30 + 20 = 50 Add units: 7 + 4 = 11 237 + 324 = 500 + 50 + 11 = 561
Bridging	Calculate 477 + 127 Split 127: 104 + 23 Bridge to 500: 477 + 23 = 500, then 500 + 104 = 604

Lesson 3: **Subtracting 2- and 3-digit numbers**

- Select and use effective strategies to subtract pairs of 2- and 3-digit numbers

Key words
- subtraction
- counting back
- partitioning
- bridging
- compensation
- compatible numbers

Number

Discover

Knowing a good mental method for subtraction is important when calculating change.

If you buy something in a shop, you can correct mistakes if you know what change to expect.

Price

Pay with…

…change given back.

Is this correct?

Learn and Example

Some mental strategies for subtraction

Name	Example
Counting back	Calculate 97 – 30 Count back in 10s, i.e. 87, 77, 67
Partioning	Calculate 744 – 431 Split 744: 700, 40 and 4 / Split 431: 400, 30 and 1 Subtract hundreds: 700 – 400 = 300 Subtract tens: 40 – 30 = 10 Subtract units: 4 – 1 = 3 300 + 10 + 3 = 313
Bridging	Calculate 584 – 188 Split 188: 184 + 4 Bridge to 400 and subtract 4: (584 – 184) – 4 = 396

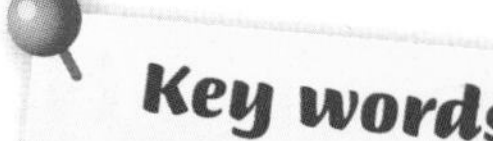

Lesson 4: **Adding more than two numbers**

- Use a written method to find the total of three or more 2- and 3-digit numbers

Key words
- place value
- estimate
- carry
- palindrome

Discover

Sometimes you need to add two or more numbers.

In a leaf count, figures reported by different groups must be added regularly to keep the count up to date.

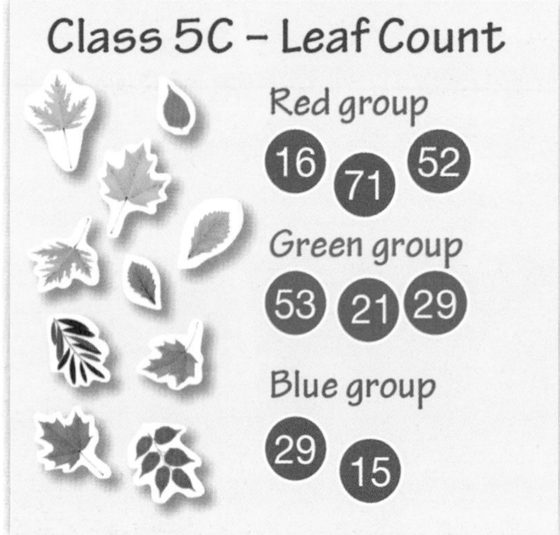

Remember, there are other written methods you can use!

Learn

In the column method, the same rules apply for adding more than two numbers as for just two.

- Align the digits into columns according to their place value.
- Draw a line under the last number and write a + sign.
- Work from right to left, column by column.
  - Add the digits in the column, including any carried digits.
  - Write each digit of the answer in the same column as the digits being added, but under the line.
  - Make a note of any carried digits in the next column to the left.

Example

Add 198, 549 and 276.

		1	9	8
		5	4	9
+		2	7	6
	1	0	2	3
		2	2	

Lesson 5: Adding and subtracting 2- and 3-digit numbers

- Select and use effective strategies to add and subtract pairs of 2- and 3-digit numbers

Key words

- counting back
- partitioning
- bridging
- compensation
- compatible numbers

Discover

Being able to calculate mentally shows a good understanding of the numbers involved. There are times when you want a quick method for solving a problem without the need for pen and paper. For example, when you want to work out the differences in packet sizes in a supermarket.

Learn and Example

Some mental strategies for subtraction

'Friendly' numbers	Numbers easily recognised as subtracting to a multiple of 5, 10, 100, …	Calculate 650 – 375 Split 375: 350 + 25 650 – 375 = 650 – 350 – 25 = 300 – 25 = 275
Compensation	Rounding the second number to a multiple of 10, 100, …, subtracting, then making an adjustment.	Calculate 783 – 399 Round 399 to 400 783 – 400 = 383 Adjust 383 up 1 to compensate for taking one too many, so 384

Workbook page 84

Lesson 6: **Adding more than two numbers**

- Use a written method to find the total of three or more 2- or 3-digit numbers

Key words

- budget
- place value
- estimate
- carry

Discover

Suppose you have to buy an amount of an ingredient for a recipe in separate quantities. It is important to add the amounts together to make sure you have enough.

If there isn't a set of scales around then you will have to rely on mental addition!

Learn

For column addition, remember that if the sum of the digits in a column is greater than 9, you must carry the higher place value digit to the next column on the left. When you add the next column, you add in the carried digit.

Example

```
     6 7 1
     4 5 8
     2 1 4
+    3 4 8
  --------
   1 6 9 1
  --------
     1 2
```

Lesson 7: **Adding decimals**

- Add pairs of 3- or 4-digit numbers, with the same number of decimal places, including amounts of money

Key words
- place value
- estimate
- carry

Number

Discover

If you buy more than two things it is a good idea to add the amounts together to make sure you have enough money to pay for them.

Before ordering at a restaurant, you can use the menu to add prices together. Then the final bill shouldn't be a surprise!

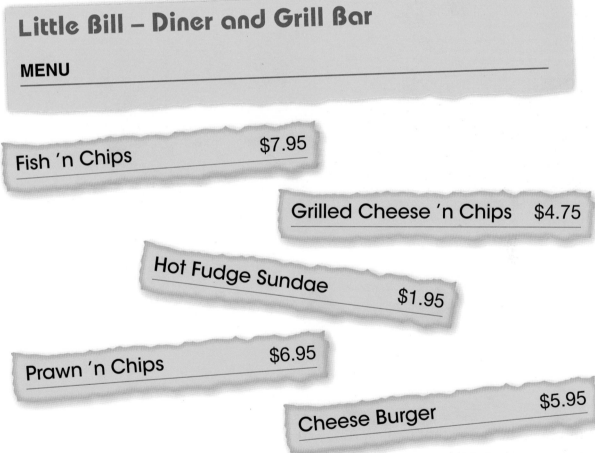

Little Bill – Diner and Grill Bar

MENU

Fish 'n Chips $7.95

Grilled Cheese 'n Chips $4.75

Hot Fudge Sundae $1.95

Prawn 'n Chips $6.95

Cheese Burger $5.95

Learn

Column addition for decimals is similar to that for whole numbers. Add the digits in each place value column. The most important thing is to make sure all the decimal points are lined up and the answer has the decimal point in the correct place.

Example

$$\begin{array}{r} 54.82 \\ +\,38.76 \\ \hline 93.58 \\ \hline {}^{1}\,{}^{1} \end{array}$$

Number

Lesson 8: Subtracting decimals

- Subtract pairs of 3- or 4-digit numbers, with the same number of decimal places, including amounts of money

Key words
- place value
- estimate
- rename (decompose)

Discover

Being able to subtract decimals is an important skill, especially when it comes to calculations involving money and measurements. For example, to save money, a restaurant may choose to reduce the amount of ingredients it uses.

Reduce by 12·65 kg

Learn

To subtract a smaller decimal number from a larger decimal number, write the larger number above the smaller number, with the decimal points lined up.

Then calculate the subtraction as you would for whole numbers and line up the decimal point in the answer.

Example

\$83.72 – \$36.49

	7 13		6 12
	~~8~~ ~~3~~	·	~~7~~ ~~2~~
–	3 6	·	4 9
	4 7	·	2 3

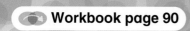

Lesson 1: **Adding and subtracting decimals mentally**

Key words
- partition
- compensation
- 'find the difference'

Number

- Use a range of strategies to add and subtract decimals mentally

Discover

Being able to add and subtract decimals mentally provides a set of tools that can be used when you need to calculate quickly – but which strategy should you use?

Look first at the problem and then decide the best method. It should be a strategy you feel comfortable using and one that gets you the answer as quickly and as easily as possible.

21·4 + 42·3
37·8 + 51·9
68·8 – 13·6
94·6 – 22·8

Learn and Examples

<table>
<tr><td>Strategy: Partitioning</td><td>Strategy: Compensation</td></tr>
<tr><td>57·4 + 2·3 = (57 + 2) + (0·4 + 0·3)
= 59·7
68·5 + 24·9 = (68 + 24) + (0·5 + 0·9)
= 92 + 1·4
= 93·4
58·7 – 42·3 = (58·7 – 42) – 0·3
= 16·7 – 0·3
= 16·4</td><td>75·3 – 31·8 = (75·3 – 32) + 0·2
= 43·3 + 0·2
= 43·5</td></tr>
</table>

Workbook page 92

Lesson 2: Adding and subtracting near multiples mentally

Key words

- compensation
- compensate (adjust)
- bridging
- jottings

- Use a range of strategies to add and subtract near multiples of 10, 100 and 1000 mentally

Discover

What do these addition and subtraction calculations have in common? They all involve addition and subtraction of near multiples of powers of 10. What strategy would you use to solve them?

44 + 18
637 + 399
7153 + 4997
87 – 19
466 – 298
8528 – 2997

Learn and Examples

Strategy: Counting on, adding in stages

46 + 38 = (46 + 30) = 76 + 8 = 84

2344 + 4503 = 2344 + 4000 + 500 + 3 = 6847

Strategy: 'Find the difference', counting on from smaller to larger number

2027 – 899

1, 100, 1000, 27
899 900 1000 2000 2027 = 1128

Strategy: Compensation

486 + 398 = (486 + 400) – 2
= 886 – 2
= 884

7384 – 5997 = (7384 – 6000) + 3
= 1384 + 3
= 1387

Lesson 3: **Adding more than two numbers**

- Use a written method to find the total of more than two numbers

Key words
- place value
- estimate
- carry

Discover

There are many situations in life where you have to add more than two numbers together.

For example, after eating in a restaurant, it is important to check the bill to make sure the price of each item has been added correctly.

Usually, the digits are lined up in place value columns making it easier to check the total!

The Happy Diner

4	Pizza	133.00
3	Salmon	139.00
1	Crab	43.00
4	Chef's Special	260.00
2	Ice cream	13.00
3	Coffee	11.00

Total: ?

****

Thank you for dining with us!

****

Learn

When you add more than two numbers in a column, use different strategies to make it easier to add. For example, look for doubles and numbers that make 10, or group the numbers in a different order to make it easier to add mentally.

Example

Add 248, 356, 172 and 486.

As 8 + 2 is 10, position 248 and 172 next to each other.

As 6 + 6 is 12, position 356 and 486 next to each other.

$$\begin{array}{r} 486 \\ 356 \\ 172 \\ +\ 248 \\ \hline 1262 \\ \hline {}_{2\ 2\ } \end{array}$$

Workbook page 96

Lesson 4: Adding and subtracting decimals

- Add and subtract pairs of 3- or 4-digit numbers, with the same number of decimal places, including amounts of money

Key words
- place value
- estimate
- carry
- rename (decompose)

Discover

Temperatures are usually given in whole numbers.

However, it is possible for temperature sensors to report temperatures with a higher accuracy, such as to the nearest tenth.

A temperature that is often given as a decimal is normal body temperature, 36·8 °C.

What is the difference between the temperatures shown on the thermometers?

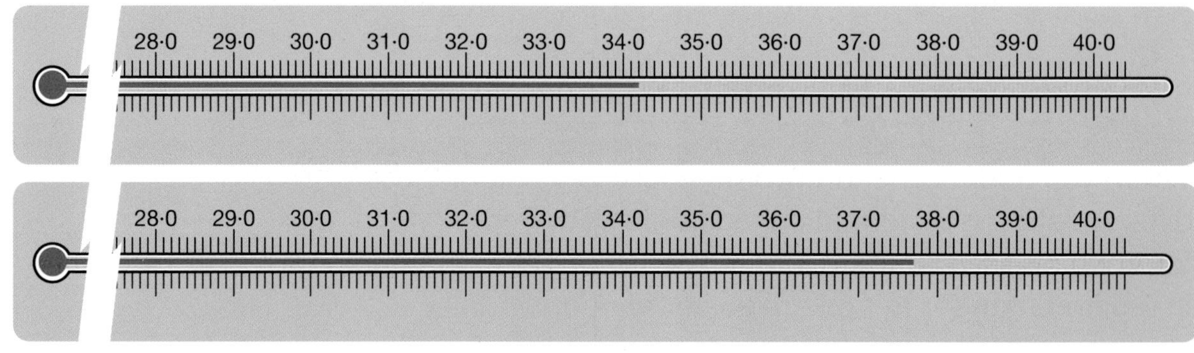

Learn

When adding and subtracting decimals remember to line up the decimal points in the two numbers before you start.

Insert zeros at the end of decimal numbers that differ in numbers of digits.

Example

$$\begin{array}{r} 4\,\overset{4}{\cancel{5}}\,.\,\overset{15}{\cancel{6}}\,{}^{1}0 \\ -\quad 1\,.\,7\,2 \\ \hline 4\,3\,.\,8\,8 \\ \hline \end{array}$$

Line up the decimal points!

Lesson 1: **Multiples**

- Recognise the multiples of 6, 7, 8 and 9
- Know whether a number is divisible by 2, 5, 10 and 100 by applying a test

Key words
- **multiple**
- **divisibility rule**

Discover

Wouldn't it be useful to know whether a number can be divided by another, without doing the calculation? The **divisibility rules** help you to do this!

Instead of doing a division, you can use the rules to say if a number can be divided without a remainder. This is particularly useful for very large numbers.

Is 83 745 divisible by 5?
Is 38 414 divisible by 2?
Is 98 330 divisible by 10?

Learn and Examples

A number is divisible by …	Example
2 if the last digit is 0, 2, 4, 6 or 8.	2462 is divisible by 2 since the last digit is 2
5 if the last digit is either 0 or 5.	7365 is divisible by 5 since the last digit is 5
10 if last digit is 0.	23 470 is divisible by 10 since the last digit is 0
100 if last two digits are both 0	43 600 is divisibly by 100 since the last two digits are 0

Lesson 2: **Factors**

- Find factors of 2-digit numbers

Key words

- multiple
- key fact
- divided by
- product
- factor

Discover

Factors are important because they can help us break things into equal groups. They help us to solve problems like the one here.

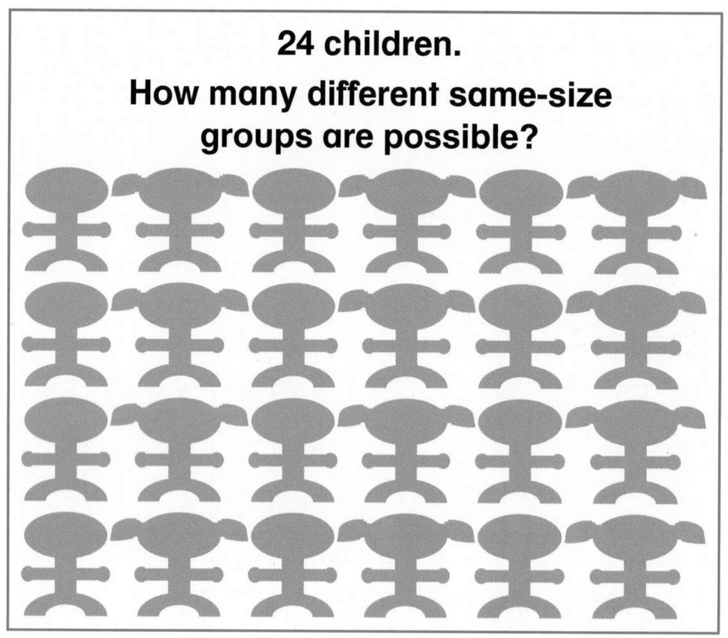

24 children.
How many different same-size groups are possible?

Learn

Factors are numbers that, multiplied together, give a larger number.

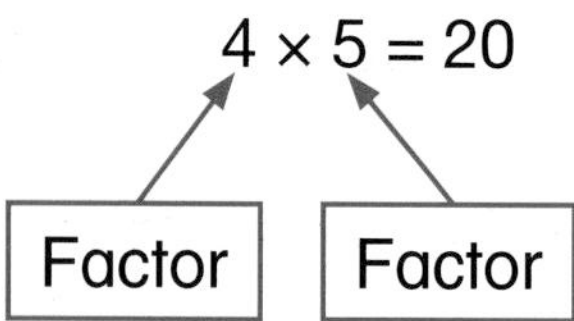

Every number has at least two factors, 1 and the number itself.

Example

12 has six factors: 1, 2, 3, 4, 6 and 12.

24 has eight factors: 1, 2, 3, 4, 6, 8, 12 and 24.

96 has twelve factors: 1, 2, 3, 4, 6, 8, 12, 16, 24, 32, 48 and 96.

Lesson 3: Multiples and factors

- Know multiplication and division facts for the 2× to 10× tables
- Identify multiples and factors, including finding all factor pairs of a number

Key words
- number fact
- multiple
- factor
- factor pair
- array

Discover

An **array** (a grid of rows and columns) is a useful model for multiplication.

In an array, the number of squares in each row represents one of the factors in the multiplication, while the number of columns represents the other factor.

The rows and columns of the arrays in the grid below show factors of 24. How would you use arrays to find all the arrangements for 36 chairs placed in different rows and columns?

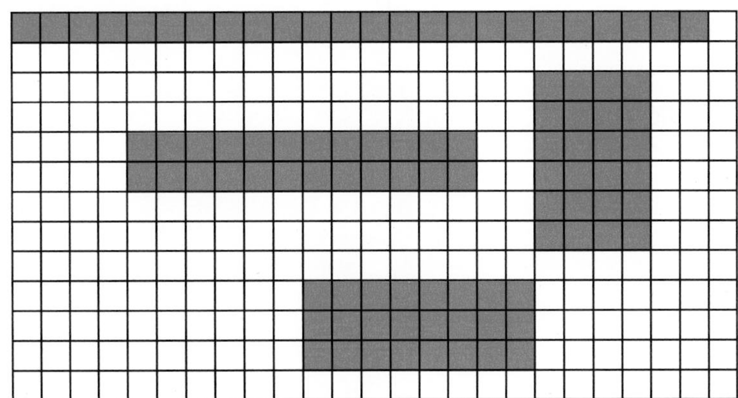

Learn

Since division is the inverse of multiplication, you can use arrays to understand how multiplication and division are related.

In multiplication, you find the product of two factors; in division you find the missing factor if you know the other factor and the product.

Example

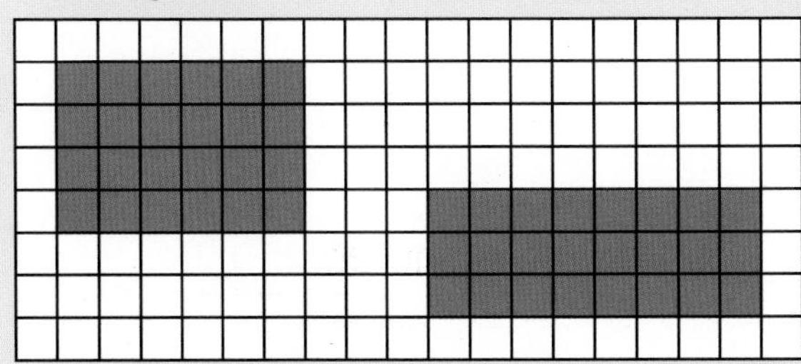

4 × 6 = 24	8 × 3 = 24
6 × 4 = 24	3 × 8 = 24
24 ÷ 4 = 6	24 ÷ 8 = 3
24 ÷ 6 = 4	24 ÷ 3 = 8

Workbook page 104

Lesson 4: Multiplying a 3-digit number by a single-digit number (1)

Key words
- multiple
- key fact
- estimate
- partition

- Multiply a 3-digit number by a single-digit number

Discover

When calculations involve larger numbers you have to decide whether to use a mental or a written strategy.

Written strategies are effective, but may not always be the quickest or most efficient way to solve a problem. Eliminate good mental strategies before deciding to use a written method.

For example, how could a farmer find the total of 3 lots of 343 sheep combined into one field?

Learn

Strategies for multiplication of a 3-digit number by a single-digit number:

a Partitioning: $378 \times 4 = (300 \times 4) + (70 \times 4) + (8 \times 4)$
$= 1200 + 280 + 32$
$= 1512$

b Grid method: 378×4

×	300	70	8	
4	1200	280	32	= 1512

c Expanded written method

```
  3 7 8
×     4
-------
    3 2
-------
  2 8 0
1 2 0 0
-------
1 5 1 2
```

Lesson 5: Multiplying a 2-digit number by a 2-digit number (1)

- Multiply a 2-digit number by a 2-digit number

Key words
- multiple
- key fact
- estimate
- partition

Discover

There are many situations in which you need to multiply a 2-digit number by another 2-digit number.

For example, a restaurant owner bought 34 chairs at $46 each. How much did he spend?

Learn

Strategies for multiplication of a 2-digit number by a 2-digit number:

a Partitioning: 78 × 63 = (70 × 63) + (8 × 63)
= 4410 + 504
= 4914

b Grid method: 78 × 63

×	70	8
60	4200	480
3	210	24

4680
+ 234
4914
1

c Expanded method:

Th	H	T	U	
		7	8	
×		6	3	
	2	3	4	(78 × 3)
4	6	8	0	(78 × 60)
4	9	1	4	
	1			

Number

Lesson 6: Multiplying a 2-digit number by a 2-digit number (2)

Key words
- doubling
- halving
- factor

- Use a halving and doubling strategy to multiply a 2-digit number by a 2-digit number

Discover

When you multiply two numbers and one is even, you can halve that number and double the other, then multiply.

You can do this over and over until you get a multiplication that's easier to solve.

Knowing how to double and halve numbers are useful skills when it comes to multiplication.

Learn

Use the strategy of doubling and halving to rewrite multiplications as simpler problems. Double one number then halve the other number.

The strategy works best when one number can be easily doubled and the other easily halved.

How many cakes?

Example

How can you work out how many cakes are in the picture?

There are 16 rows and 14 columns.

$$
\begin{aligned}
14 \times 16 &= 28 \times 8 \\
&= 56 \times 4 \\
&= 112 \times 2 \\
&= 224
\end{aligned}
$$

There are 224 cakes.

Lesson 7: **Dividing a 3-digit number by a single-digit number (1)**

- Use mental strategies to divide a 3-digit number by a single-digit number

Key words
- key fact
- divide
- divisible by
- estimate
- partition

Discover

Knowing how to divide a 3-digit number by a 1-digit number is an important skill, particularly when dealing with money.

Say, for example, a shopper wants to know if a 'buy-three-for' supermarket offer is good value for money. They would convert the total price to cents, then divide it by 3 and compare it to the price of a single item.

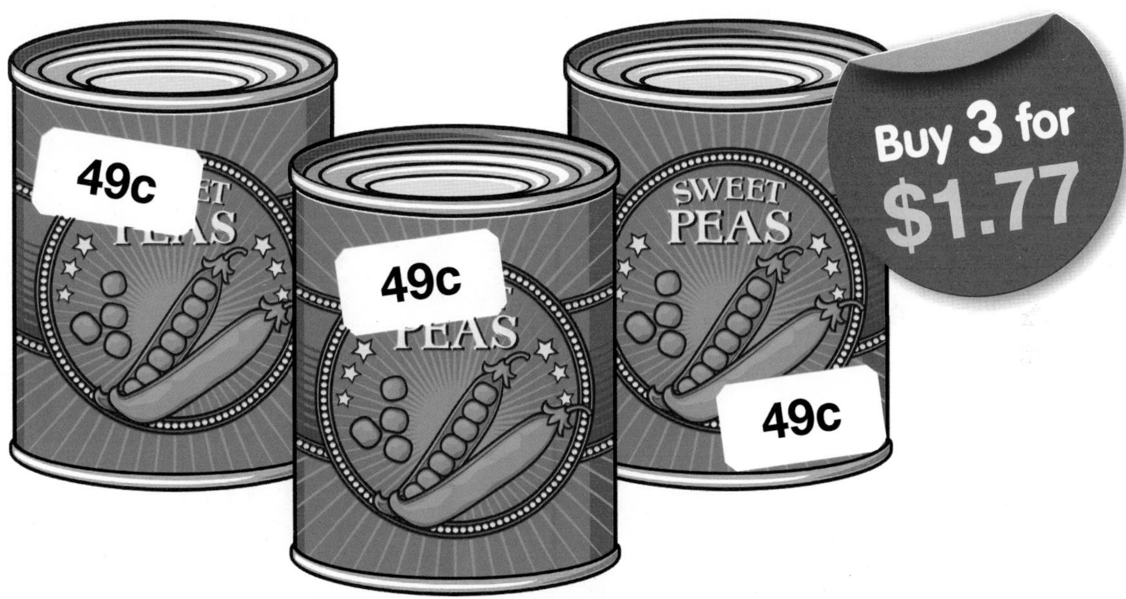

Learn

You can use known facts to help you divide a 3-digit number by a 1-digit number.

Example

For division facts, think multiplication! If you are trying to solve 270 ÷ 9 you would say: '9 times **what** is 27?' This is 3. If 9 times 3 makes 27, then it follows that 9 times 30 would make 270.

Lesson 8: **Dividing a 3-digit number by a single-digit number (2)**

- Use mental and written strategies to divide a 3-digit number by a single-digit number

Key words
- key fact
- divide
- divisible by
- estimate
- grouping
- sharing

Discover

Given a division problem, you have to decide whether to use sharing or grouping.

Consider this problem: $270 is split among 3 people. How much will each person receive?

This is a sharing problem: $270 shared equally among 3 gives $90 each. But given a different problem you might use grouping.

For example, split $396 among 9 people. It is easier to think 'How many sets of 9 make 396?' even though the problem is not about groups of 9, but about 9 groups.

Learn

The expanded written method for division involves repeated subtraction of multiples of the number we divide by.

Example

		3	6	r 4
8	2	5	2	
−	2	4	0	(30 × 8)
		1	2	
−			8	(6 × 8)
			4	

Lesson 1: **Multiplication and division facts**

- Know multiplication and division facts for the 2× to 10× tables
- Know squares of all numbers to 10 × 10

Key words
- multiplication table
- multiplication
- division
- fact family
- fact triangle

Number

Discover

The triangle shows a **fact family**, three numbers related by multiplication and division.

The answer to the multiplication is at the top and the numbers that are multiplied are at the bottom.

If the top number is divided by one of the bottom numbers, the answer is the other bottom number.

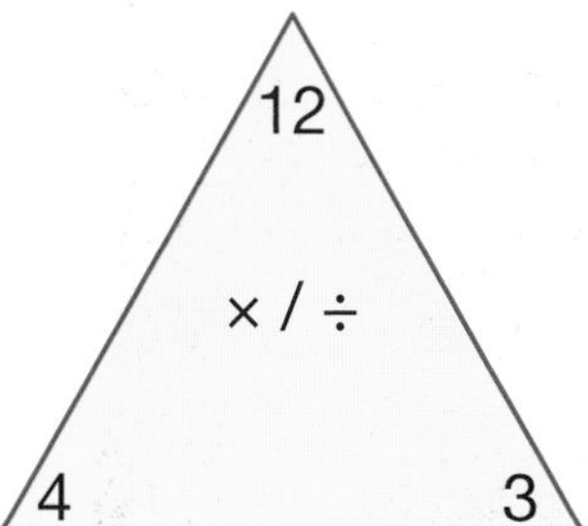

Learn

Use fact triangles to practise multiplication.

Cover the largest number and say both multiplication facts. For a triangle showing 12, you would say, '4 × 3 = 12' as well as '3 × 4 = 12'.

To practise division, show the largest number and cover up one of the smaller numbers.

Example

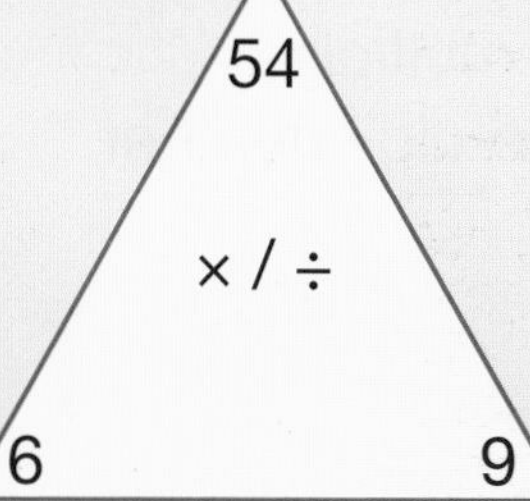

6 × 9 = 54

54 ÷ 6 = 9

9 × 6 = 54

54 ÷ 9 = 6

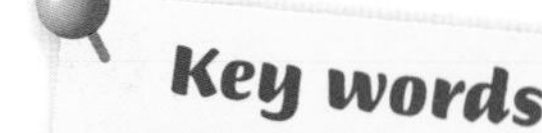
Workbook page 116

Number

Lesson 2: **Multiplying multiples of 10 and 100 (1)**

- Multiply multiples of 10 to 90, and multiples of 100 to 900, by a single-digit number

Key words
- number fact
- multiple
- partition
- place value

Discover

A hotel is hosting three different parties, for 30, 60 and 90 people. Each person attending needs three drinks, six items of cutlery and eight small chocolates.

How would you work out the total number of drinks, items of cutlery and chocolates required by each party?

Learn

You can use knowledge of number facts and place value to multiply multiples of 10 to 90, and multiples of 100 to 900, by a single-digit number.

Example

$90 \times 7 = 10 \times 9 \times 7$
$= 10 \times 63$
$= 630$

$700 \times 6 = 100 \times 7 \times 6$
$= 100 \times 42$
$= 4200$

Lesson 3: **Multiplying by 19, 21 or 25 (1)**

Key words
- multiple
- round
- adjust

- Multiply by 19 or 21 by multiplying by 20 and adjusting
- Multiply by 25 by multiplying by 100 and dividing by 4

Number

Discover

Eight groups of 20 people plan to visit a zoo. What would happen if one person in each group dropped out?

You can find the number of people going by using the fact that one group of eight are not going. Rather than multiplying by 19 (the number now going in each group), you multiply by 20 and subtract 8. This is an example of an 'adjusting' strategy.

Learn

To multiply:

- by 19: multiply by 20 and subtract the number
- by 21: multiply by 20 and add the number
- by 25: multiply by 100 and divide by 4. Dividing by 4 is equivalent to halving, then halving again.

Example

$8 \times 19 = (8 \times 20) - 8$
$= 160 - 8$
$= 152$

$6 \times 21 = (6 \times 20) + 6$
$= 120 + 6$
$= 126$

$12 \times 25 = (12 \times 100) \div 4$
$= 1200 \div 4$
$= (1200 \div 2) \div 2$
$= 600 \div 2$
$= 300$

Number

Lesson 4: **Multiplication by factors (1)**

Key words
- multiple
- factor

- Use factors to multiply

Discover

Arrays for 12 show that 12 has three factor pairs: 1 and 12, 2 and 6, and 3 and 4. Knowing these pairs can help you rewrite calculations to make them simpler.

For example: 24 × 12 can be expressed as 24 × 3 × 4, which can then be expressed as 24 × 3 × 2 × 2.

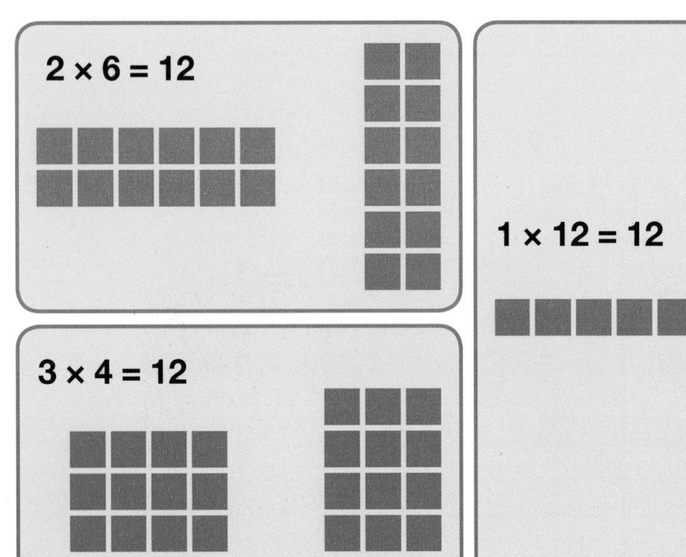

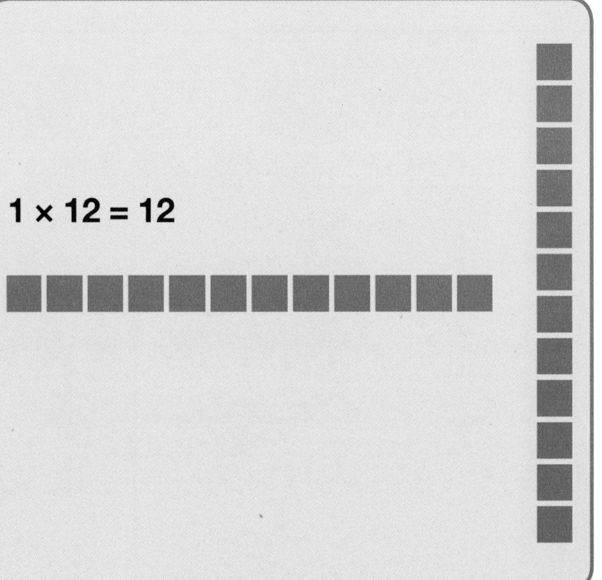

Learn

We can use knowledge of factors to express multiplication calculations in different ways.

Example

45 × 12 = 45 × 3 × 4
= 45 × 3 × 2 × 2
= 45 × 2 × 2 × 3
= 90 × 6
= 540

Knowing factor pairs makes multiplication easier!

Lesson 5: **Doubles and halves (1)**

Key words
- doubling
- halving
- inverse

- Double any number up to 100 and halve even numbers to 200
- Double multiples of 10 to 1000 and multiples of 100 to 10 000

Number

Discover

The game of 'Guess my number' helps you to understand the relationship between doubling and halving.

If you are given the answer to a doubling question then you find the number that was doubled by halving the answer.

What number is the boy thinking of?

I am thinking of a number. If I double it the answer is 124. What is my number?

Learn

Some numbers are tricky to double and half.

Partitioning can help to simplify doubling and halving problems.

Example

79 × 2 = (70 × 2) + (9 × 2) = 140 + 18 = 158

From this, we know that 790 × 2 = 1580 and 7900 × 2 = 15 800

168 ÷ 2 = (160 ÷ 2) + (8 ÷ 2) = 80 + 4 = 84

From this, we know that 1680 ÷ 2 = 840

Lesson 6: **Multiplying a 3-digit number by a single-digit number (2)**

Key words
- multiple
- key fact
- estimate
- partition

- Multiply a 3-digit number by a single-digit number using a range of strategies, including partitioning, grid and expanded written methods

Discover

It is useful to know one efficient written method of calculation for multiplication that you can rely on when mental multiplication is too difficult.

Learn

The expanded written method builds on the mental methods you have worked with.

The method involves lining up digits in place-value columns and multiplying place values by a common multiple.

Example

What is 7 multiplied by 9? (63) Write 63 in the correct place-value column.

What is 60 multiplied by 9? (540) Write 540 underneath 63.

What is 400 multiplied by 8? (3200) Write 3200 underneath 540.

Add 63, 540 and 5400, using the formal written method of addition.

Add the digits in each column starting from units, being sure to add any numbers carried over.

	6	6	7
×			9
		6	3
	5	4	0
5	4	0	0
6	0	0	3
1	1		

Lesson 7: **Multiplying a 2-digit number by a 2-digit number (3)**

Key words

- multiple
- key fact
- estimate
- partition

Number

- Use a range of strategies, including partitioning, grid and expanded written methods, to multiply a 2-digit number by a 2-digit number

Discover

You can use 2-digit by 2-digit multiplication to calculate the number of boxes stacked in layers.

Count the number in each layer (width in boxes multiplied by length in boxes) then multiply by the height in boxes.

If the boxes pictured were stacked 27 high with layers of 7 by 9, how many boxes would there be altogether?

Learn

The expanded written method builds on the mental methods.

Example

Work out 89 × 66.

What is 89 multiplied by 60? (5340)

Write 5340 in the correct place-value columns.

What is 89 multiplied by 6? (534) Write 534 below 5340.

Add 5340 and 534.

Add the digits in each column, starting from units.

		8	9
×		6	6
5	3	4	0
	5	3	4
5	8	7	4

Number

Lesson 8: **Dividing a 3-digit number by a single-digit number (3)**

- Use a range of strategies, including partitioning, grouping and expanded written methods, to divide a 3-digit number by a single-digit number
- Recognise when to round up or down after division, depending on the problem

Key words
- key fact
- estimate
- partition
- grouping
- sharing
- rounding

Discover

240 apples need to be packaged in boxes that hold 52 apples each.

How many full boxes will there be? Answer: 4. You ignore the remainder, 32 apples, and round down.

How many boxes will be needed to hold all the apples? Answer: 5. The remaining 32 apples need a box of their own. You consider the remainder and round up.

Learn

For a normal division calculation, you usually just state the remainder.

For worded problems you often need to round the answer.

Example

A coach can take 56 people. 300 people wish to travel.

a How many coaches are needed?

$300 \div 56 = 5 \text{ r } 20$

The remainder is people who still need a coach!

Round up. 5 r 20 becomes 6, so 6 coaches are needed.

b How many coaches will be full?

20 people do not make a full coach. Ignore the remainder, round down: 5.

Lesson 1: Multiply multiples of 10 and 100 (2)

- Multiply multiples of 10 to 90, and multiples of 100 to 900, by a single-digit number

Key words
- number fact
- multiple
- partition
- place value

Number

Discover

Being able to multiply multiples of 10 or 100 is a useful skill for checking the reasonableness of answers to other multiplication questions.

For example, what is 796 × 4? To estimate the answer, round 796 to the nearest 100 and multiply. So, what is 800 × 4? You know 8 × 4 = 32, so 800 × 4 is 3200.

You can use this estimate to check your answer to 796 × 4 (3184).

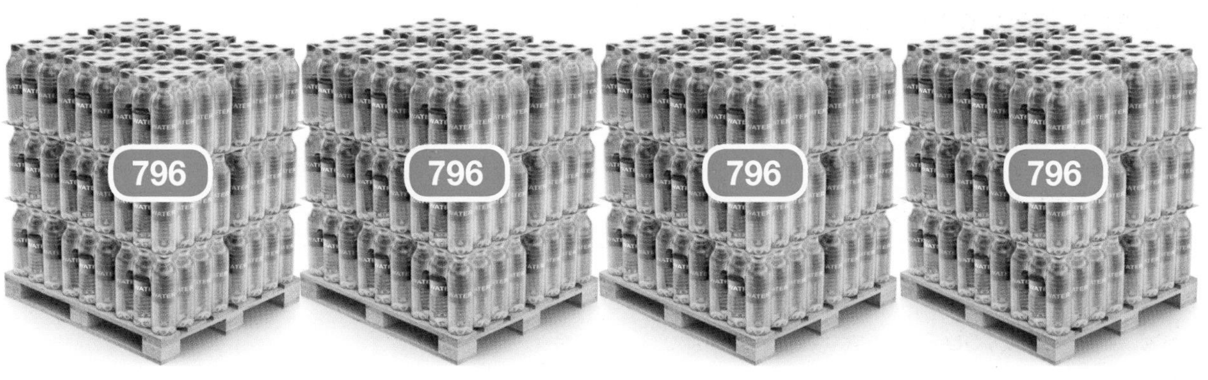

Learn

You can use a related 1-digit problem to help answer a problem that has the same digits multiplied by a power of ten.

Example

80 × 6 = 10 × 8 × 6
= 10 × 48
= 480

900 × 4 = 100 × 9 × 4
= 100 × 36
= 3600

Workbook page 132

Lesson 2: **Multiplying by 19, 21 or 25 (2)**

Key words
- multiple
- round
- adjust

- Multiply by 19 or 21 by multiplying by 20 and adjusting
- Multiply by 25 by multiplying by 100 and dividing by 4

Discover

Tins of beans are priced 80c. What is the cost of 21 tins?

You can use a simple strategy to calculate this. Find the cost of 20 tins and add the cost of 1 tin. Use the strategy to work out the cost.

Learn and Example

Number strategies for multiplying by 19, 21 or 25:

$30 \times 19 = (30 \times 20) - 30$
$= 600 - 30$
$= 570$

$70 \times 21 = (70 \times 20) + 70$
$= 1400 + 70$
$= 1470$

$60 \times 25 = (60 \times 100) \div 4$
$= 6000 \div 4$
$= 6000 \div 2 \div 2$
$= 3000 \div 2$
$= 1500$

Lesson 3: **Multiplication by factors (2)**

- Use factors to multiply

Key words
- multiple
- factor
- prime number

Number

Discover

Arrays for 6 show that 6 has two factor pairs: 1 and 6, and 2 and 3.

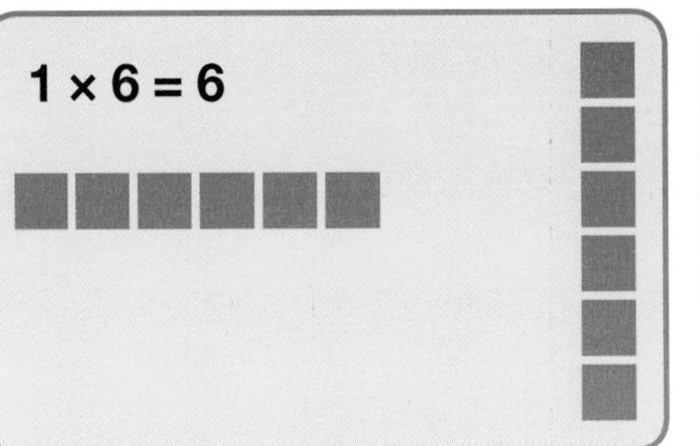

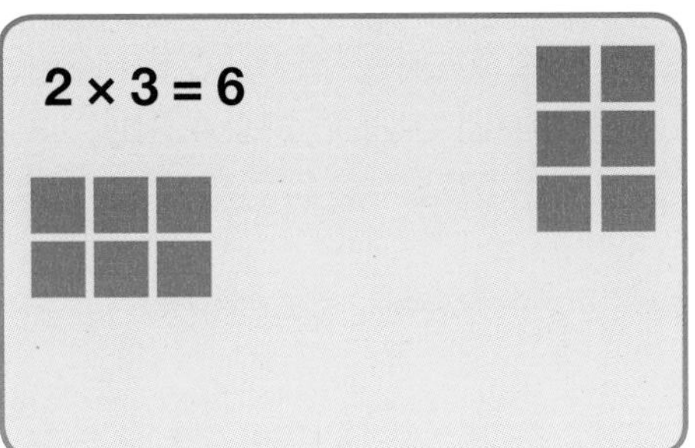

Knowing that 2 and 3 is a factor pair of 6 helps us to multiply by 6: simply multiply by 3 and double the answer.

For example, 22 × 6 can be expressed as 22 × 3 × 2 = 66 × 2 = 132.

Learn

We can use knowledge of factors to find doubles that help us to multiply numbers.

Example

12 × 14 = 12 × 7 × 2
= 84 × 2
= 168

35 × 16 = 35 × 4 × 4
= 140 × 2 × 2
= 280 × 2
= 560

I know that 4 × 4 is 16
and can double twice to
get the answer.

Workbook page 136

Lesson 4: **Doubles and halves (2)**

Key words
- doubling
- halving
- inverse

- Double multiples of 10 to 1000 and multiples of 100 to 10 000

Discover

You can use a set of halves or doubles to find related facts.

If you know double 3 is 6, then you also know double 30 is 60, double 200 is 400 and double 2000 is 4000.

Also, if you know half 70 is 35, then you also know half 700 is 350 and half 7000 is 350.

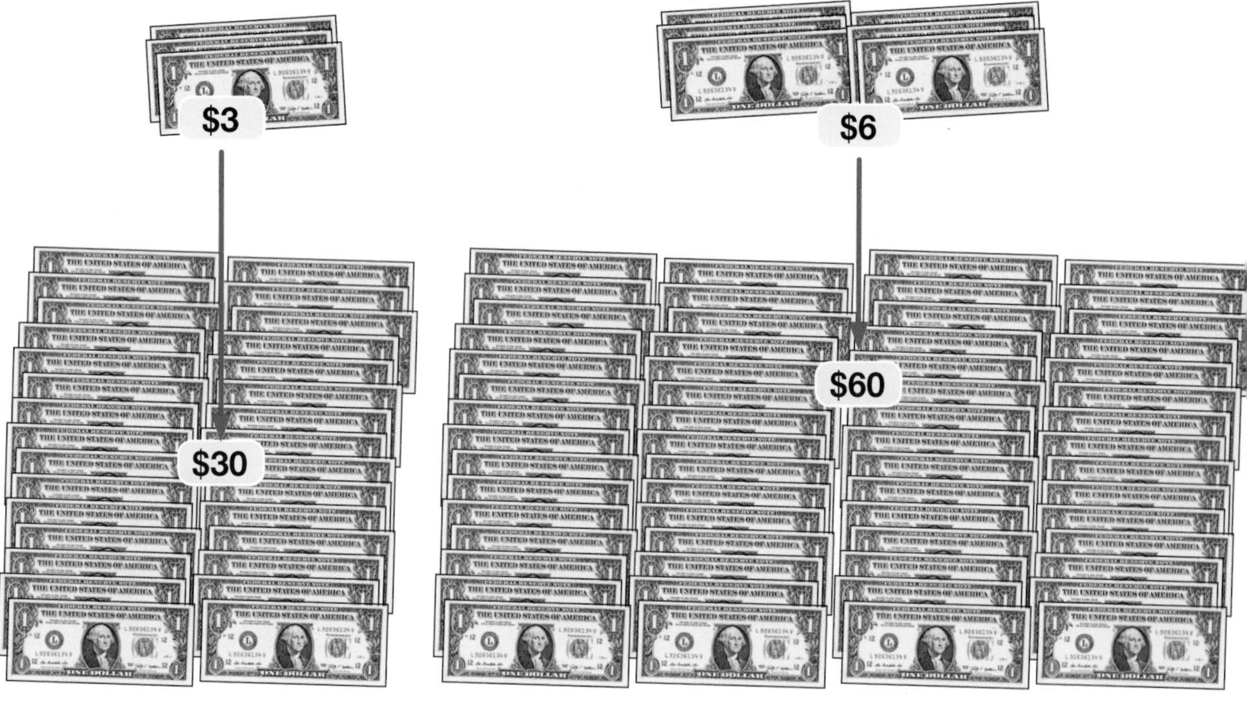

Learn

You can use place value to find sets of doubles and halves.

Example

Double 8 is 16, so: double 80 is 160, double 800 is 1600, etc.

Half 18 is 9, so: half 180 is 90, half 1800 is 900, etc.

Lesson 1: Triangles

- Identify equilateral, isosceles and scalene triangles

Key words
- equilateral
- isosceles
- scalene
- regular
- irregular
- right angle

Discover

There are three types of triangle.

equilateral

isosceles

scalene

Learn

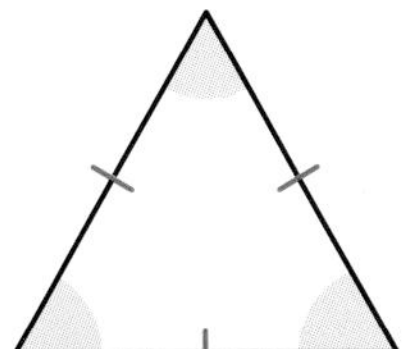

An **equilateral** triangle has 3 equal sides and 3 equal angles.

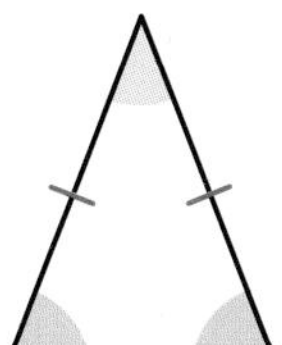

An **isosceles** triangle has 2 equal sides and 2 equal angles.

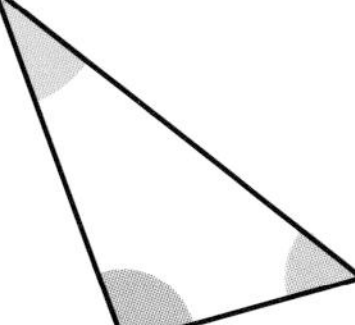

A **scalene** triangle has no equal sides and no equal angles.

Example

Equilateral triangles

Isosceles triangles

Scalene triangles

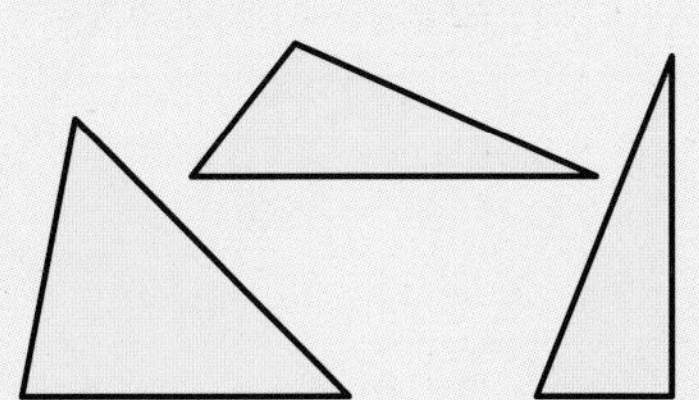

Workbook page 148

Lesson 2: Symmetry in regular polygons

- Recognise reflective symmetry in a regular polygon
- Identify lines of symmetry in a regular polygon
- Recognise rotational symmetry in a regular polygon

Key words
- reflective symmetry
- rotational symmetry
- line of symmetry
- mirror line
- regular polygon

Discover

Symmetry can be found all around you.

Learn

Reflective symmetry: both halves match as if seen in a mirror. The dividing line is called the 'line of symmetry'.

Rotational symmetry: can be rotated around its centre so it fits on top of itself in more than one way.

Example

A regular hexagon has six lines of symmetry.

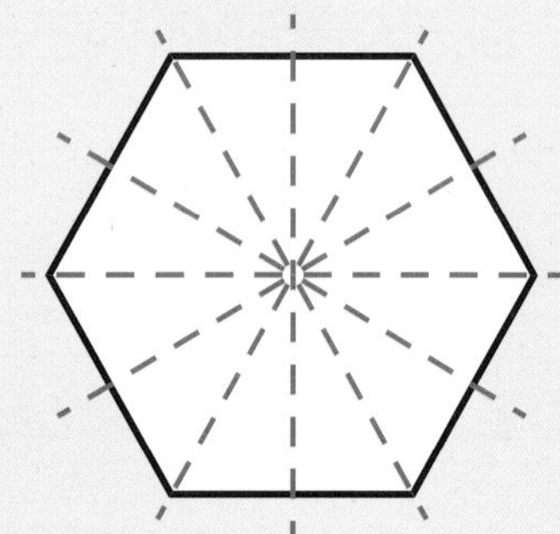

A pentagon fits on top of itself in five ways.

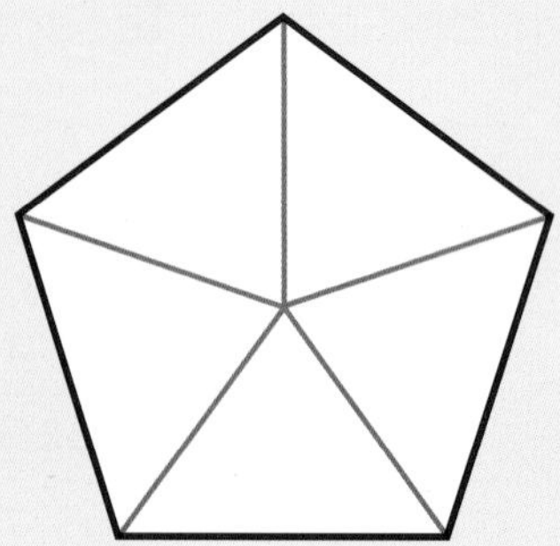

Lesson 3: **Symmetrical patterns**

- Complete a symmetrical pattern on squared paper that has two lines of symmetry

Key words
- reflective symmetry
- line of symmetry
- mirror line
- image

Discover

What do you notice about these floor mosaics?

Learn

Some patterns have one line of reflective symmetry. Some have two lines of reflective symmetry, at right angles to each other.

Example

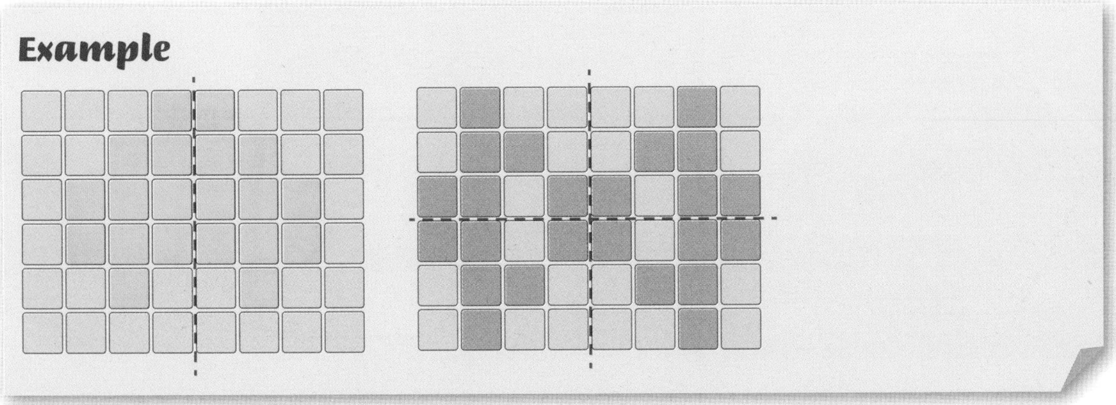

Workbook page 152

Lesson 4: **Perpendicular and parallel lines**

Key words
- parallel lines
- perpendicular lines
- right angle

- Describe parallel and perpendicular lines and recognise them in grids, shapes, and the environment

Geometry

Discover

What do you notice about the red lines in each picture?

Learn

Lines are parallel if they run in the same direction, keep the same distance apart and never meet.

Lines are perpendicular if they meet at a right angle.
The line AB is perpendicular to the line CD.

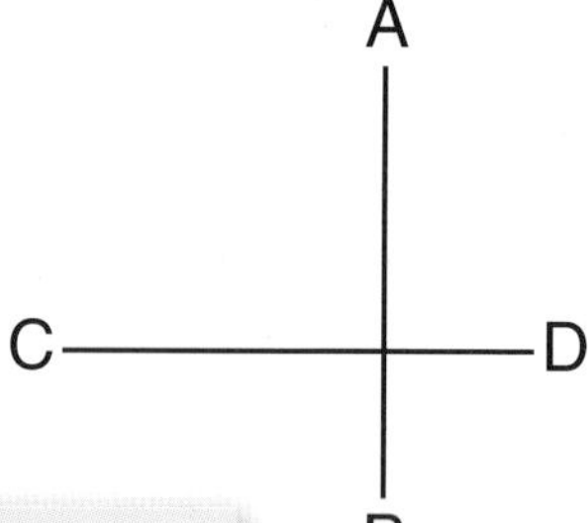

Example

Lesson 1: **Visualising 3D shapes**

- Imagine what a 3D shape would look like from a 2D drawing

Key words
- face
- edge
- vertex
- vertices

Discover

Identify the 3D shapes from their 2D drawings.

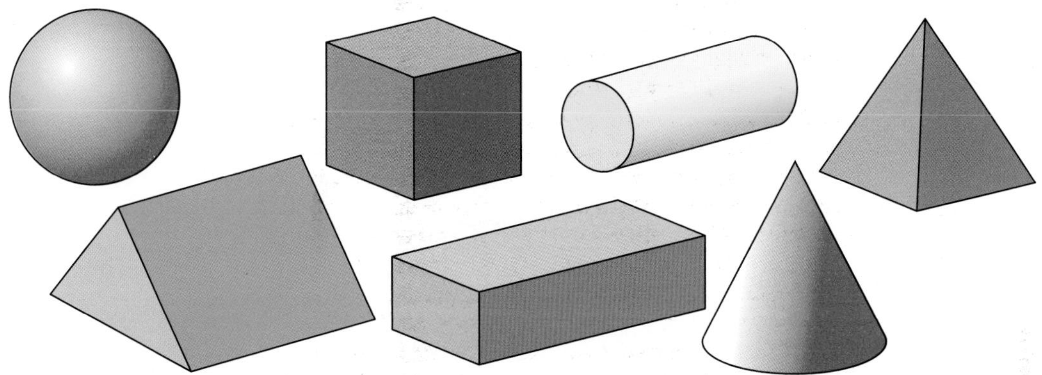

Learn

Through drawings we can represent a 3D object on a 2D surface. Dotted lines can be used to show the edges and faces we would not be able to see.

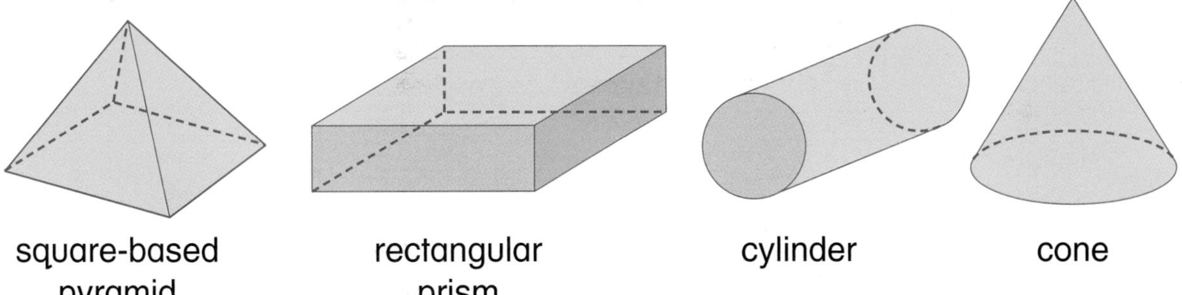

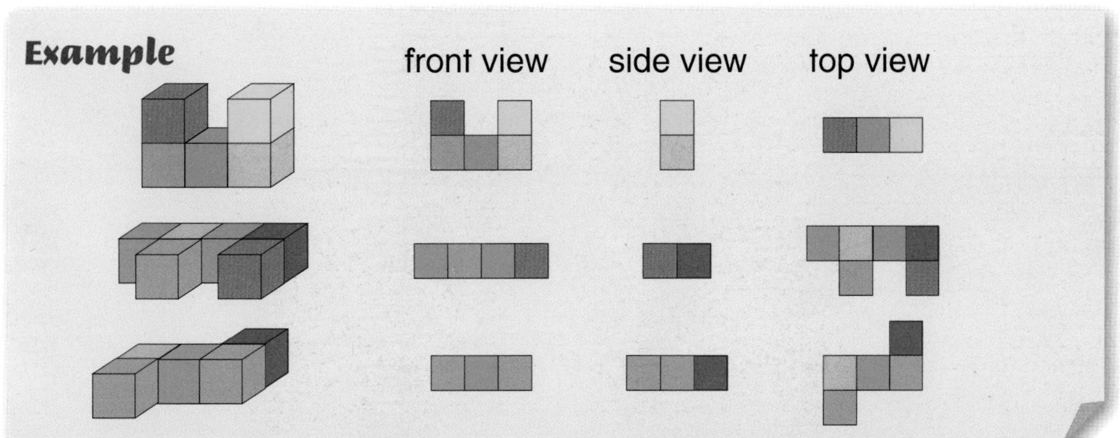

Lesson 2: **Nets**

- Imagine what a 3D shape would look like from its net
- Identify and build different nets for a cube
- Identify a net that will not produce a cube

Key words
- face
- net
- open cube
- closed cube
- vertex

Geometry

Discover

A net is a flat shape that can be folded to make a 3D shape.

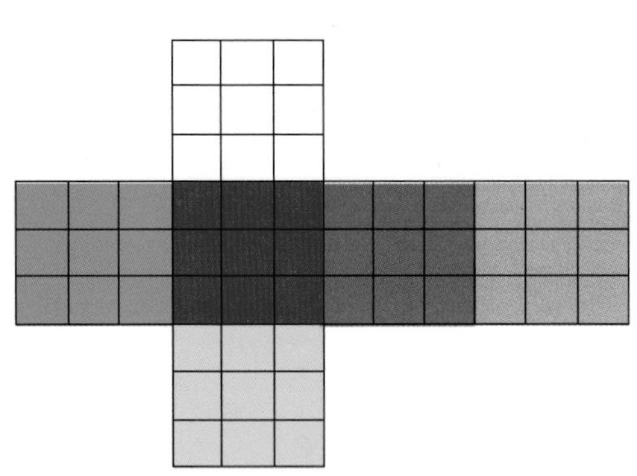

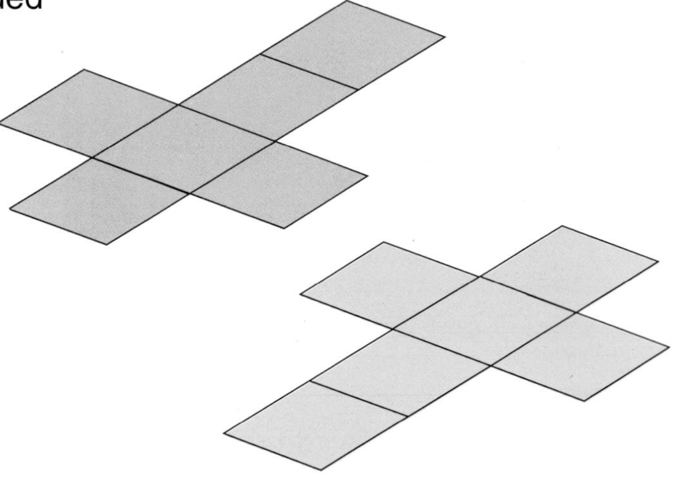

Learn

Nets show which parts are the base, top and sides when folded up.

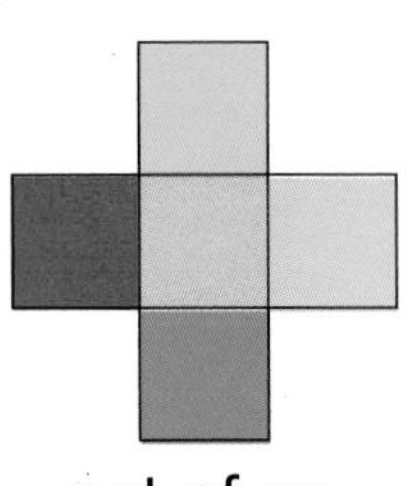

net of an open cube

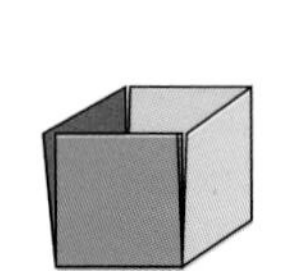

open cube (folded)

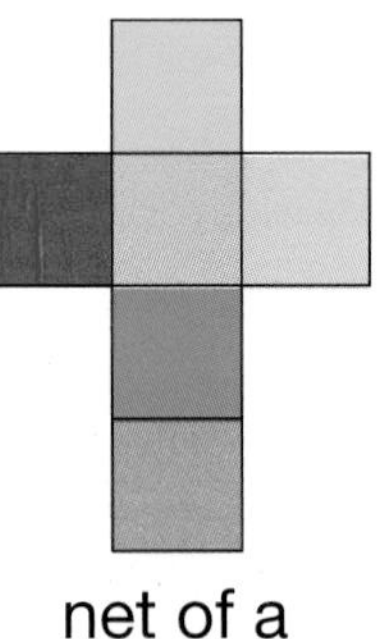

net of a closed cube

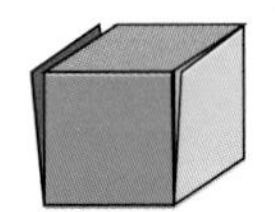

closed cube (folded)

Example

There may be several nets for one shape, for example, a closed cube:

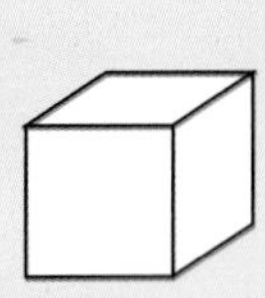

Lesson 3: **Constructing 3D shapes**

- Build 3D shapes from different materials
- Build and use skeleton shapes to spot edges and vertices

Key words
- pyramid
- prism
- octahedron
- face
- vertex
- edge
- skeleton

Discover

The skeleton of a 3D shape shows edges and vertices clearly.

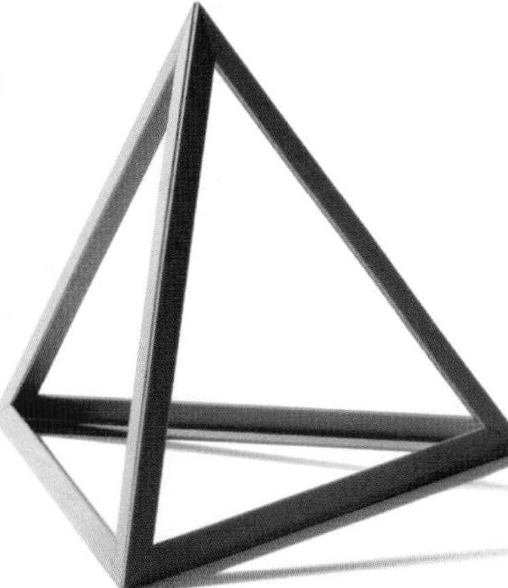

Geometry

Learn

A cube has 6 square faces, 8 vertices and 12 edges.

A cuboid has 6 rectangular faces, 8 vertices and 12 edges.

A pentagonal prism is a prism with two pentagonal faces parallel to each other. It has 7 faces, 10 vertices and 15 edges.

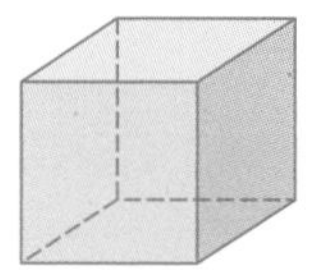
cube

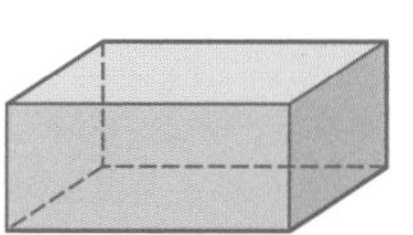
cuboid

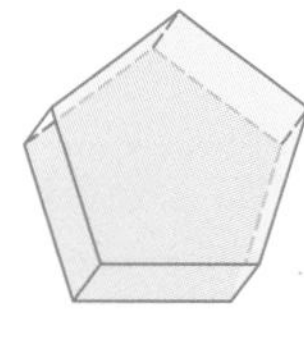
pentagonal prism

Example

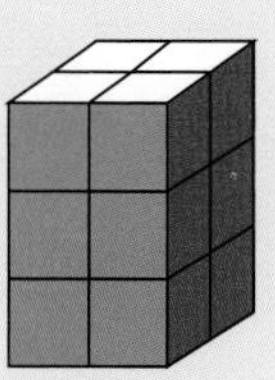

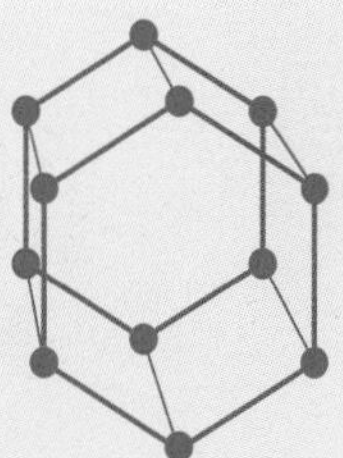

Lesson 4: **Relationships between 3D shapes**

Key words
- net
- vertex
- face
- edge
- point (apex)

- Know that prisms and pyramids are named according to the shape of their base
- Recognise the relationships between different 3D shapes

Geometry

Discover

You can sort 3D shapes into sets according to their properties. What properties are common to all prisms? All pyramids?

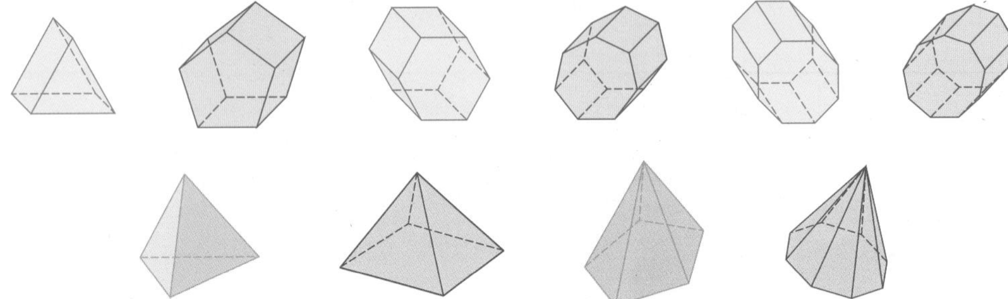

Learn

Pyramids are named after the shape of their base.

Their sloping sides join at a point.

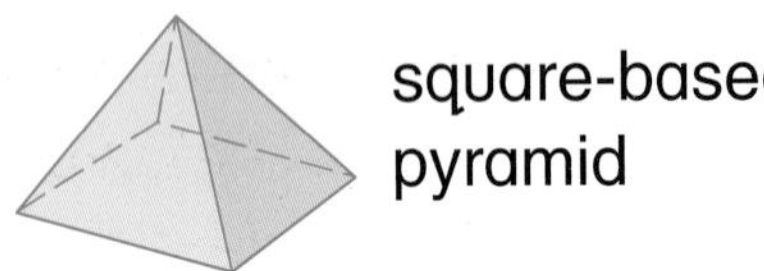

square-based pyramid

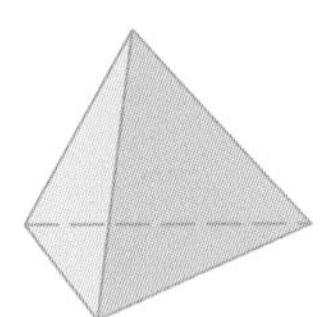

triangular-based pyramid

Prisms are named after the shape of the identical faces at each end.

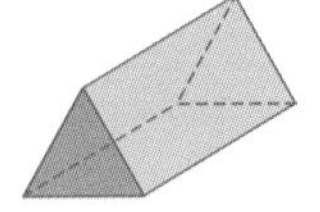

triangular prism

rectangular prism

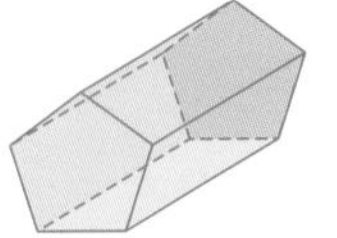

pentagonal prism

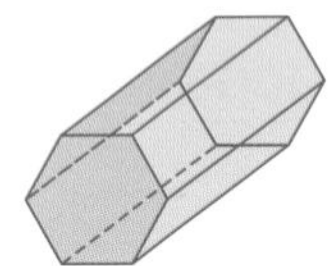

hexagonal prism

Example

square-based pyramid

triangular prism

hexagonal prism

Lesson 1: **Measuring angles**

- Know how to use a protractor to measure an angle
- Measure an angle to the nearest 5°

Key words
- angle
- protractor

Discover

A pizza slice is like a sector of a circle – the greater the angle at the centre, the larger the slice.

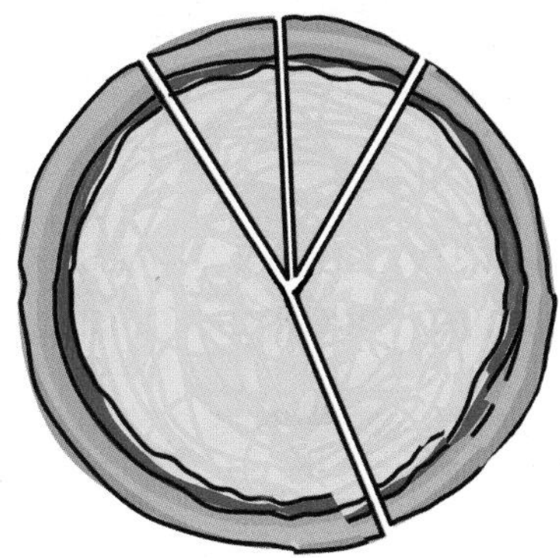

Learn

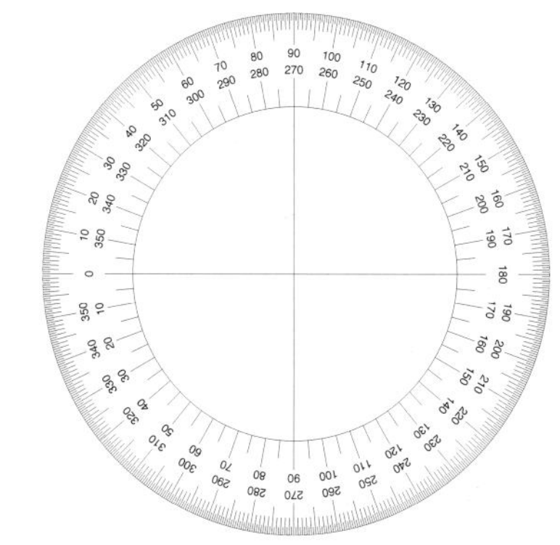

Degrees (angles)

360° = Full rotation

180° = Half rotation

90° = Quarter turn (right angle)

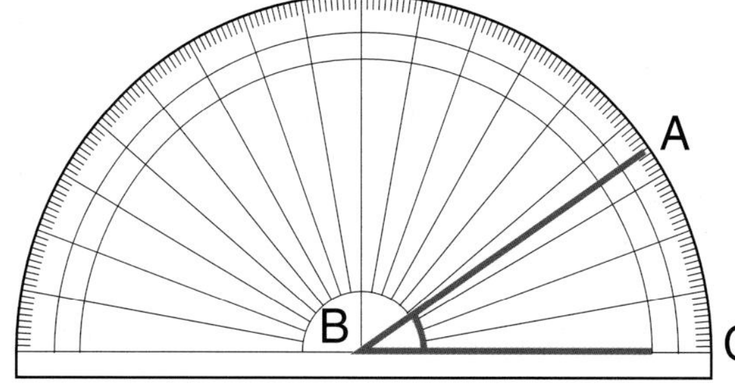

Measuring degrees

Use a protractor with its centre point on vertex B and 0° (base line) over the arm of the angle (AC). Measure the angle between the arms.

Example

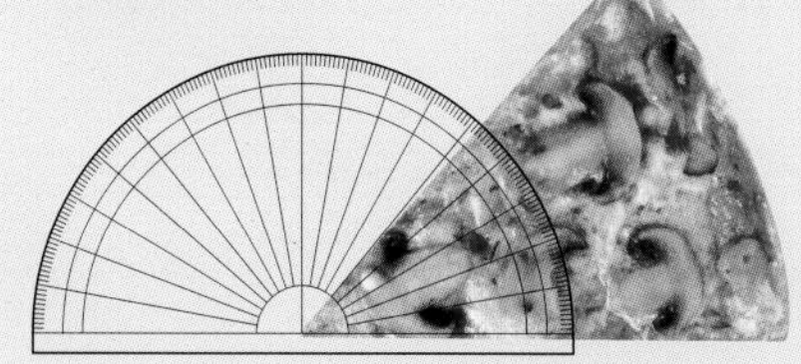

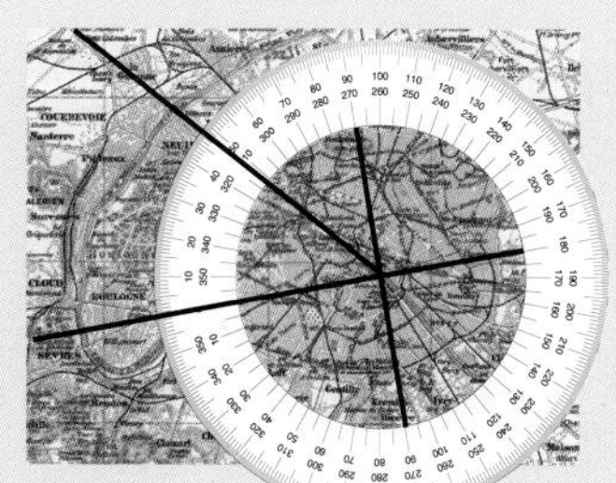

Lesson 2: **Angle size**

- Identify and describe angles less than, equal to or greater than a right angle (90°)
- Estimate the size of an angle and place angles in order

Key words
- right angle
- straight angle
- degrees

Geometry

Discover

An angle is made between hands on a clock face. As the hands move, the angle changes.

Learn

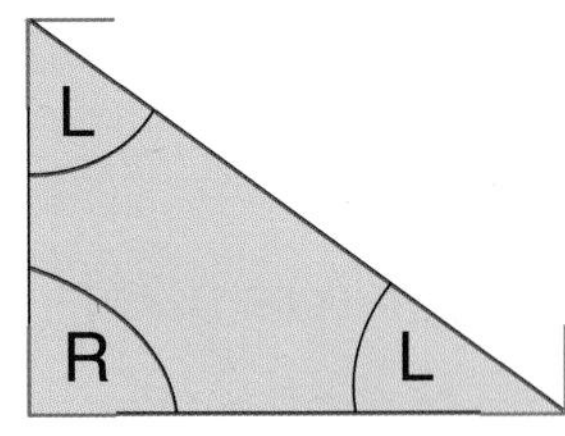

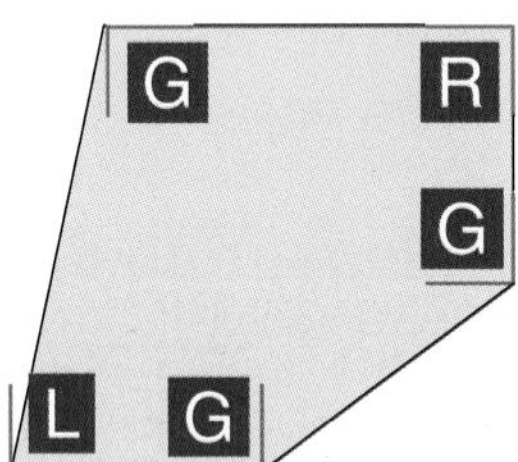

We can compare angles as:
L = less than a right angle (90°)
R = right angle (90°)
G = greater than a right angle (90°)

We can compare angles.

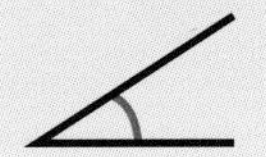 is less than  is greater than 

Ascending order 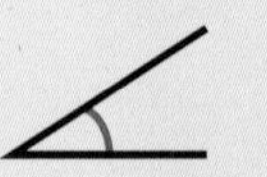 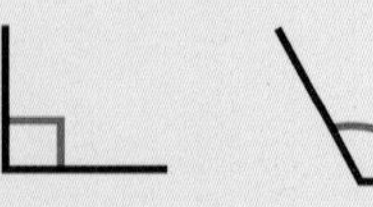  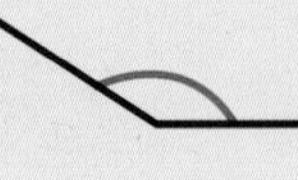

Descending order 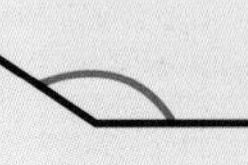 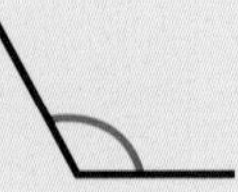 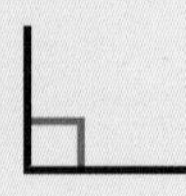 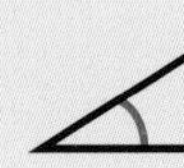

Lesson 3: **Classifying angles**

- Classify angles as right angle, acute or obtuse

Key words
- right angle
- acute angle
- obtuse angle

Geometry

Discover

Which is the best angle to hang the painting?

Learn

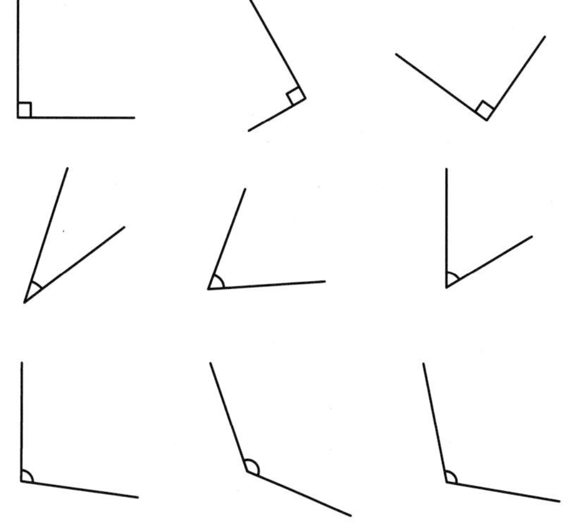

Right angle

Angle of 90°. Its symbol is a little square box.

Acute angle

Angle less than 90°.

Obtuse angle

Angle greater than 90° but less than 180°.

Example

Lesson 4: **Angles on a straight line**

- Identify two angles at a point on a straight line

Key words
- right angle
- straight angle
- angles at a point

Geometry

Discover

Angles that meet on a straight line always add up to 180°.

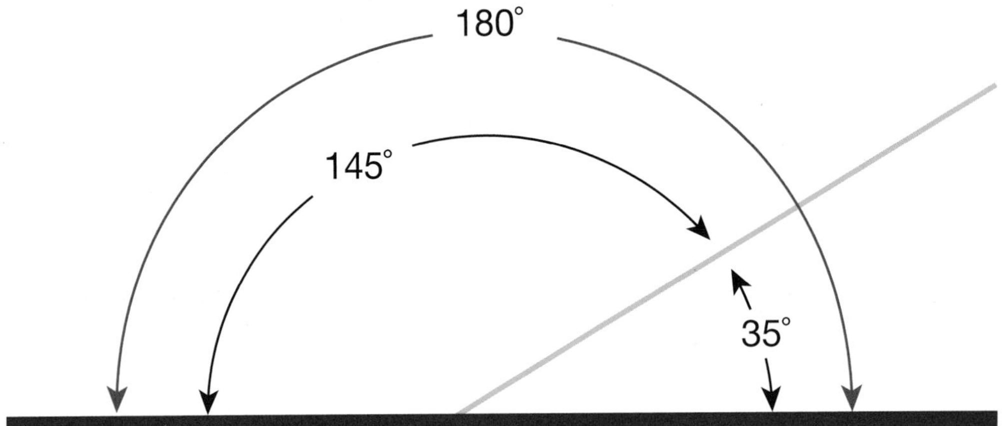

Learn

Missing angles

If you know one of two angles that meet at a point on a straight line, then you can easily work out the other angle.

You can use your knowledge of addition and subtraction strategies, such as counting on, to work out the answer.

Example

180° – 131° = 49°

So the missing angle is 49°.

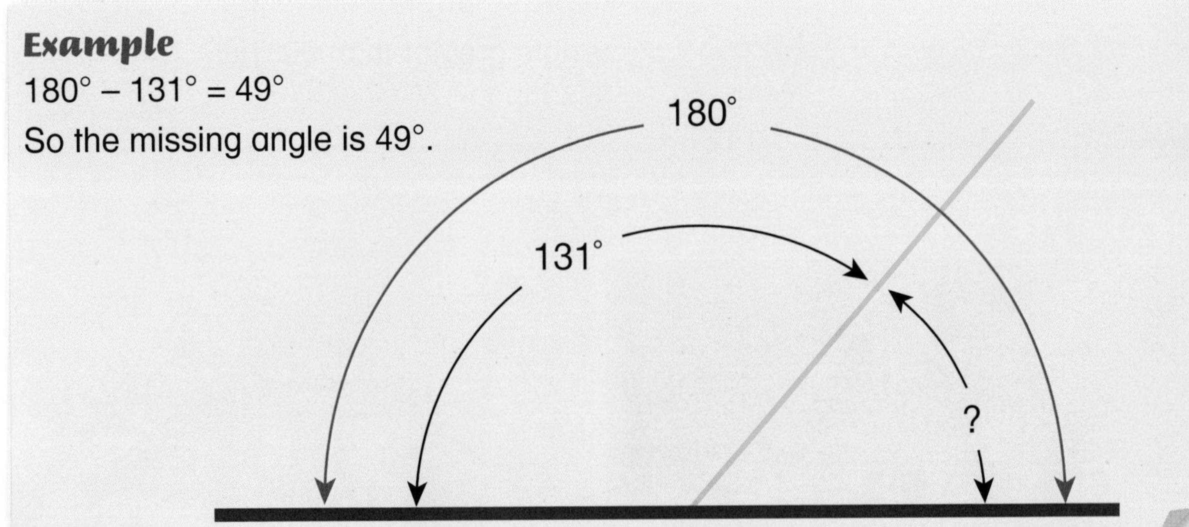

Lesson 1: **Reading and plotting co-ordinates**

- Understand that co-ordinates show the exact position of a point on a grid

Key words
- *x*-axis
- *y*-axis
- co-ordinates
- origin

Discover

The position of any object in the real world can be described using a numbered grid system.

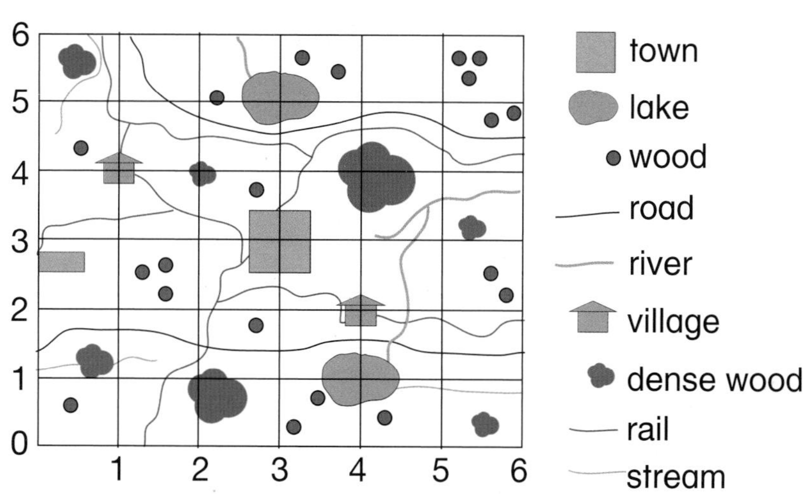

Learn

Co-ordinates pinpoint a point on a graph or map. The numbers are written in brackets separated by a comma, for example, (1, 6). The first number shows how many places to move across the horizontal axis; the second number shows how many places to move up the vertical axis.

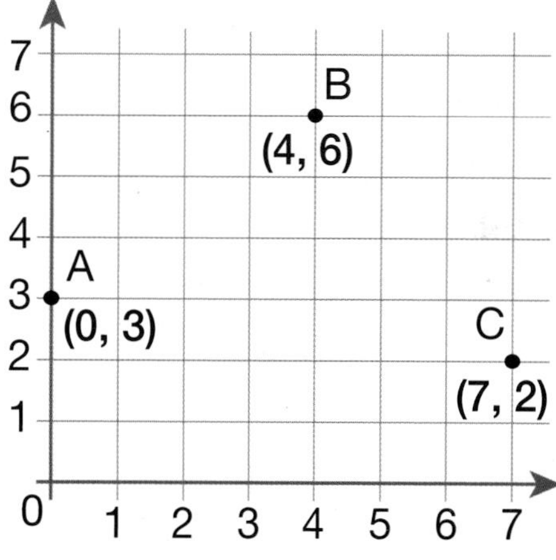

Example

Plot the point (2, 3).

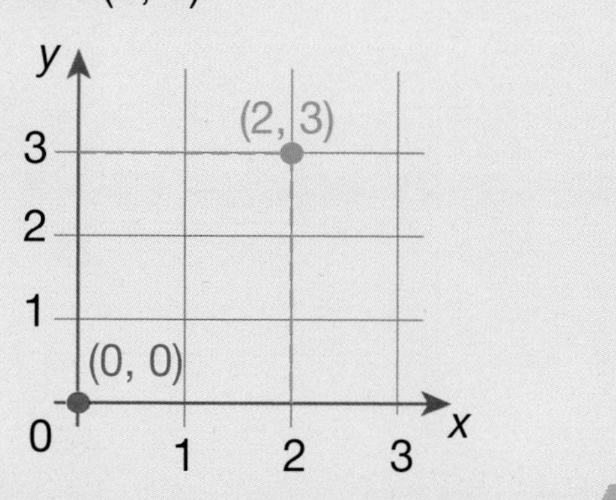

Workbook page 172

Lesson 2: **Shapes from co-ordinates**

- Plot specific points on a co-ordinate grid to form a shape

Key words
- *x*-axis
- *y*-axis
- co-ordinates
- vertex (vertices)

Geometry

Discover

The coordinates of the vertices of the pink rectangle are: (1, 5), (3, 5), (3, 1), (1, 1).

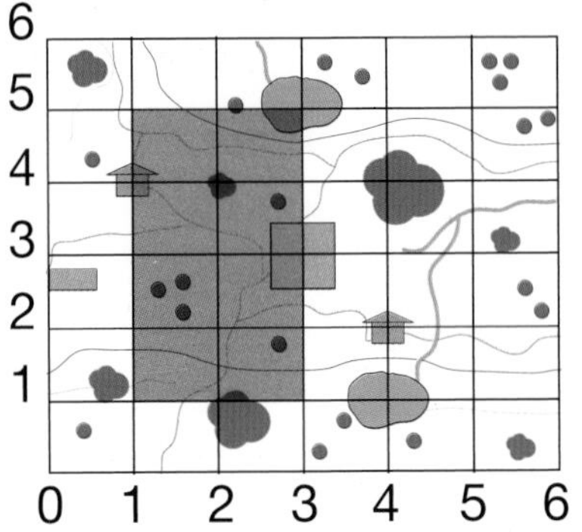

Learn

You can use co-ordinates to plot and draw shapes. Points corresponding to vertices are plotted and connected.

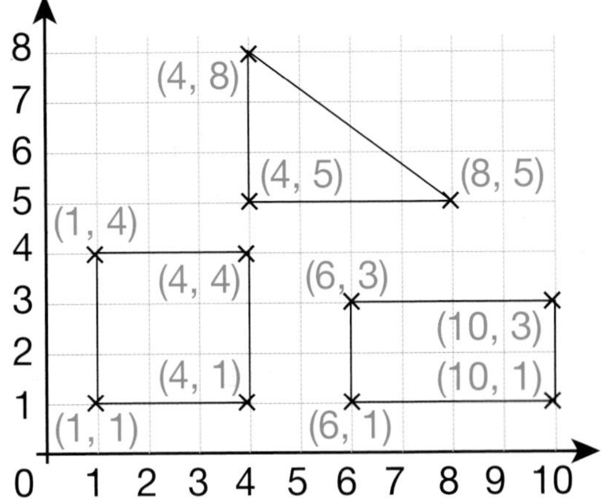

Example

Knowing the co-ordinates of parts of a shape may help you to find the co-ordinates of any missing vertex.

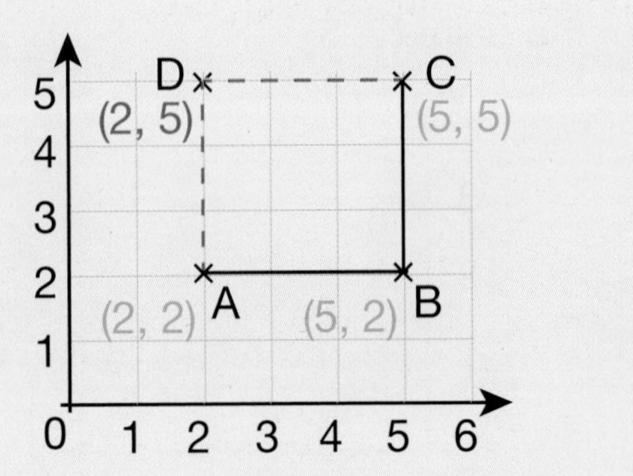

Lesson 3: Testing for symmetry

- Fold paper shapes or use mirrors to test shapes for symmetry

Key words
- line of symmetry
- mirror line
- reflection
- symmetrical
- horizontal
- vertical

Discover

Symmetry can be found everywhere – from manmade patterns to nature. It can be explained by mathematics.

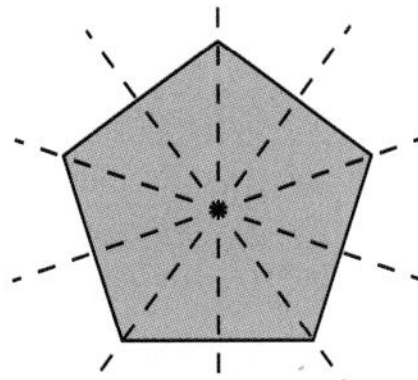

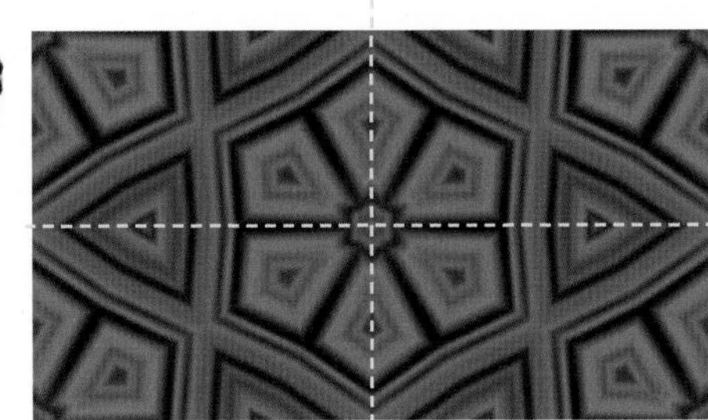

Learn

If you can fold a shape so that one half matches the other exactly, then the shape is symmetrical.

fold → unfold →

line of symmetry

Place a mirror along each line to see if the shape you see in the mirror is the same as the original.

Some shapes may look symmetrical but, in fact, are not.

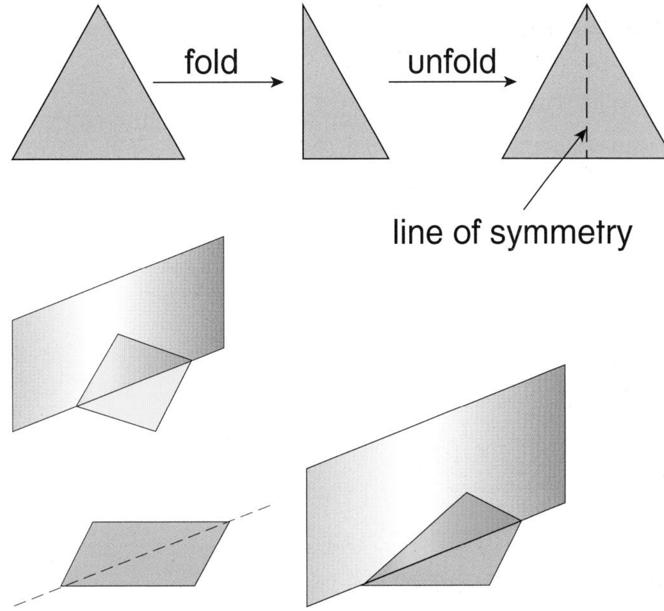

Example

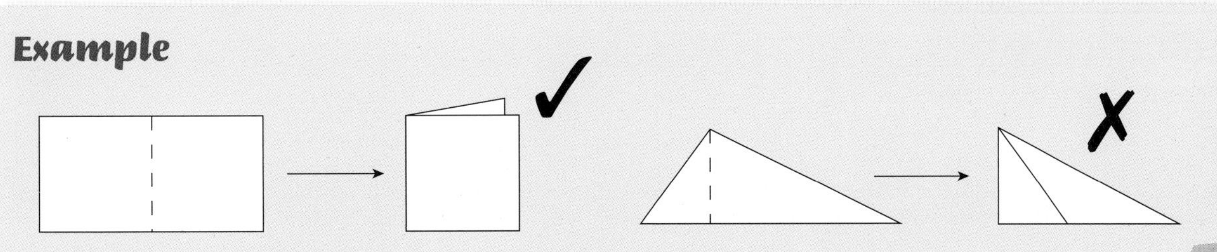

Geometry

Workbook page 176

Lesson 4: **Reflection (1)**

- Identify and describe the position of a shape following a reflection

Key words
- reflection
- image
- line of symmetry
- parallel
- vertex (vertices)

Discover

Reflections are all around you. You will have seen mirror-like reflections in a water surface, or your own reflection in a mirror.

Learn

In a reflection, a point moves to a new position an equal distance from the mirror line, but on the other side. This distance is always measured at right angles to the mirror line.

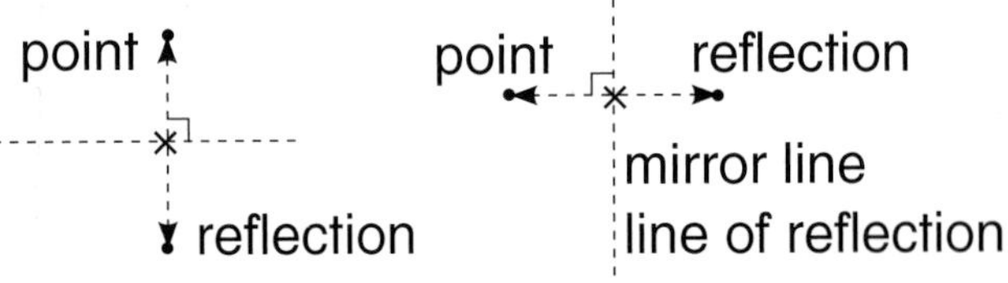

Each vertex of the shape moves across the mirror line to a point the same distance from the line, but on the opposite side of the line of symmetry. The original shape is called the object and its reflection is called the image.

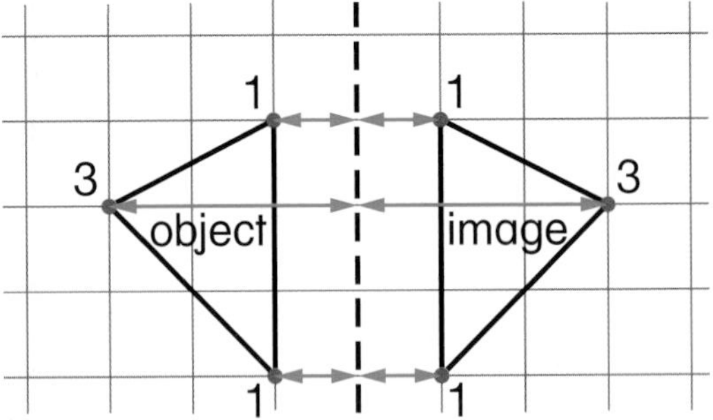

Example

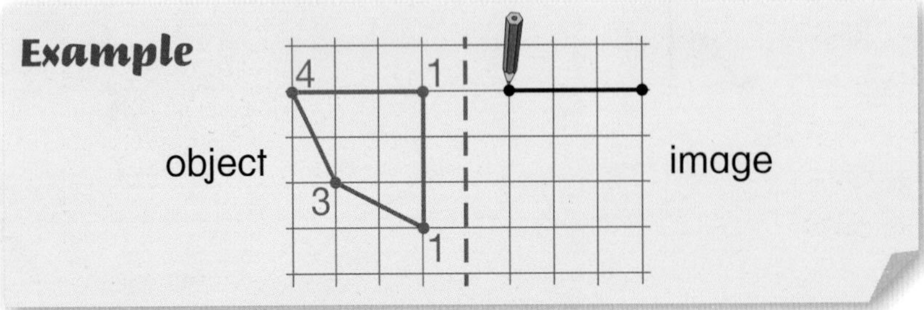

Lesson 5: **Reflection (2)**

- Predict and draw where a shape will be after reflection where the mirror line is not vertical or horizontal

Key words
- reflection
- image
- mirror line
- oblique
- right angle

Discover

Reflections can take place across surfaces that are at an angle to the horizontal.

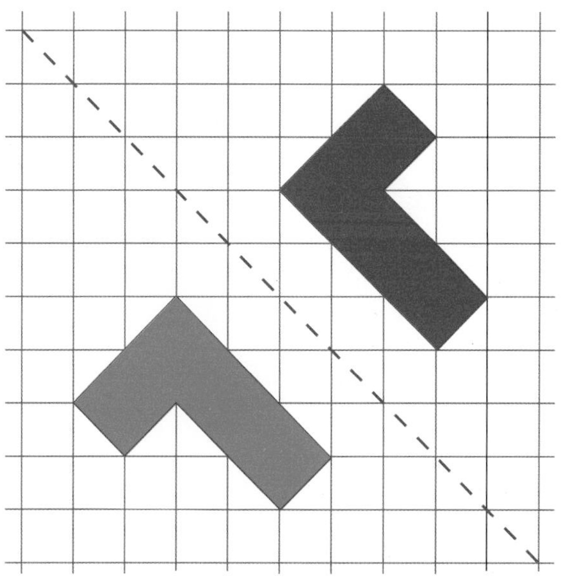

Learn

Mirror lines can go in any direction.

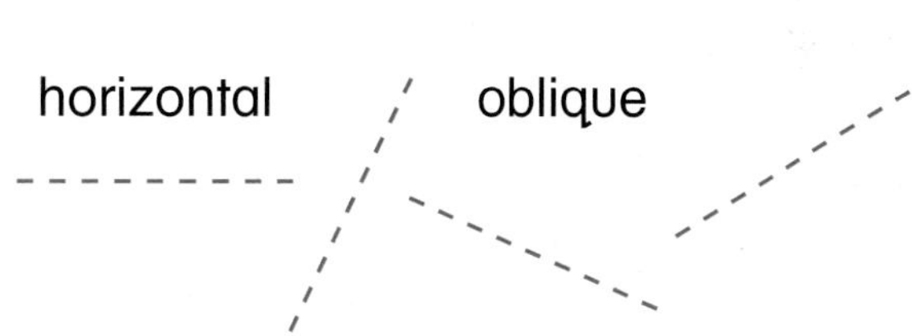

Reflecting a shape across an oblique mirror line has the same rules as reflecting a shape across a vertical or horizontal mirror line. Measure the perpendicular (at right angles to) distance from each vertex to the mirror line. Measure the same distance again on the other side of the line and place a dot. Finally, join the dots to form the image.

Example

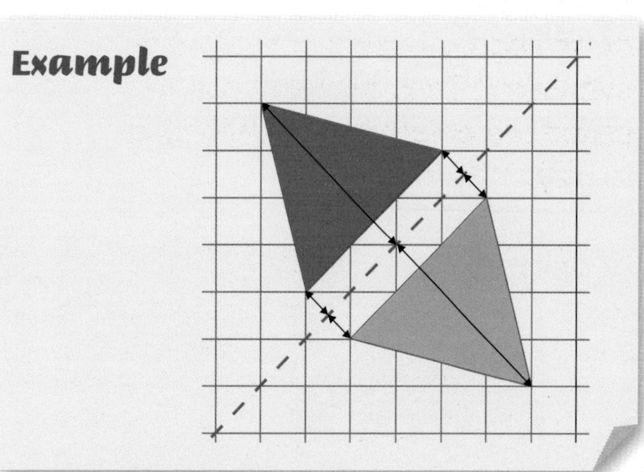

Lesson 6: **Understanding translation**

- Identify, describe and represent the position of a shape after a translation

Key words
- translate
- translation
- orientation
- vertex (vertices)
- tiling pattern

Geometry

Discover

Translations can be seen in many places, from architecture to nature. You can experience translations yourself!

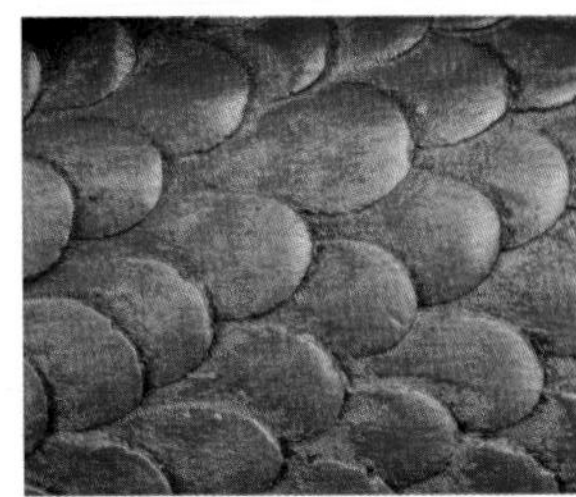

Learn

A translation is the movement of an object in a straight line. It can be moved up, down, left or right, but you can't rotate, stretch or change it.

Each vertex must move in the same direction and by the same amount. The object and its image are identical in shape, size and orientation.

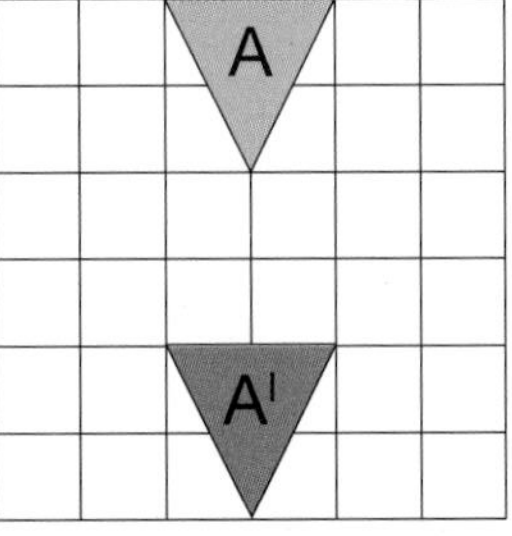

Shape A has been translated 4 squares down.

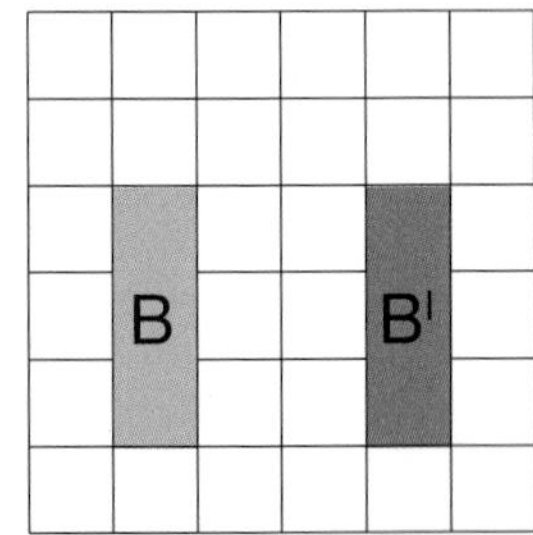

Shape B has been translated 3 squares to the right.

Example

Square ABCD has been translated 3 squares to the right.

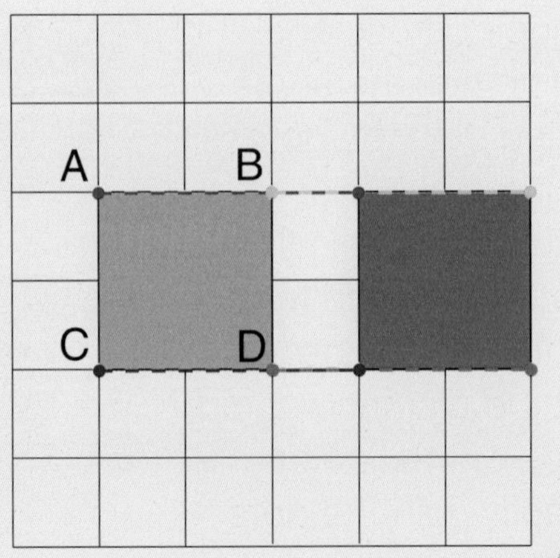

Lesson 7: **Shape translation (1)**

- Know where a shape will be after a translation and know that the shape has not changed

Key words
- translate
- translation
- orientation
- vertex (vertices)
- tiling pattern

Discover

Tiling patterns are created by translating shapes a fixed distance in a given direction. They are often used to decorate walls and floors.

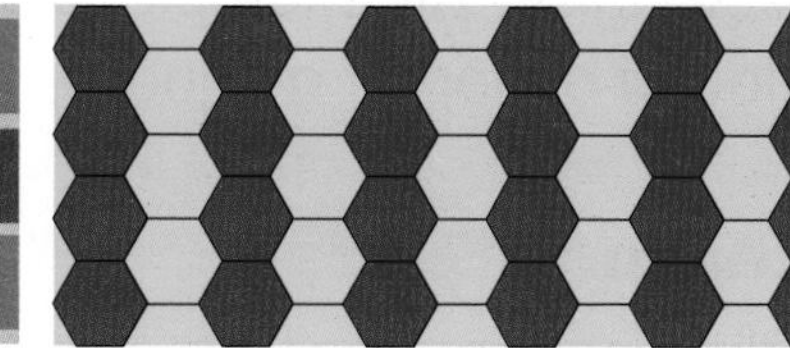

Learn

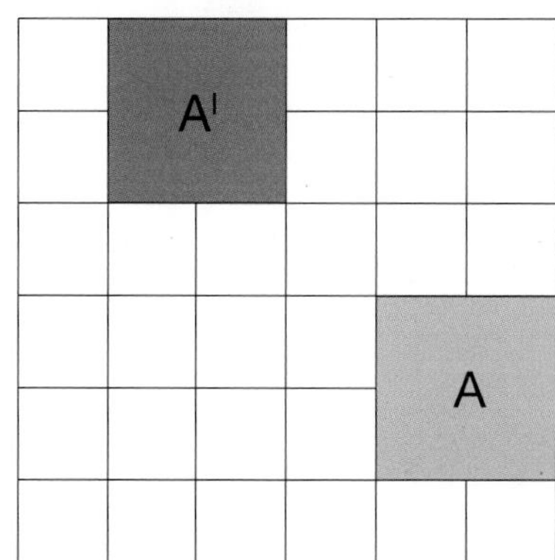

Shape A has been translated 3 squares up and 3 squares to the left.

When you translate an object, every vertex moves in the same direction, by the same amount. The object and its image are identical in shape, size and orientation.

Example

Triangle ABC has been translated 3 squares up, 2 squares right.

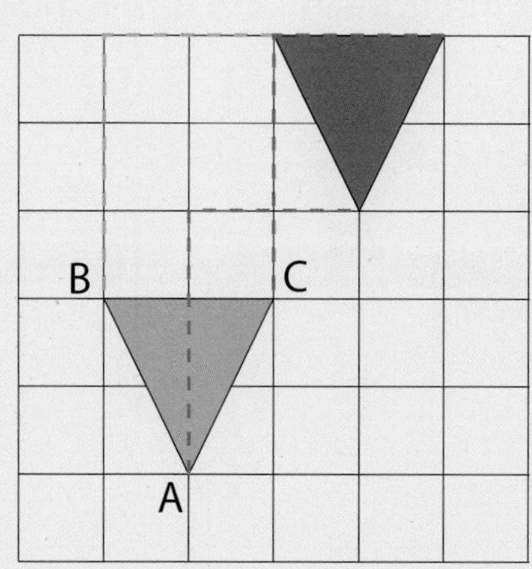

Workbook page 184

Lesson 8: **Shape translation (2)**

- Know where a compound shape will be after two translations

Key words
- translate
- translation
- compound shape
- unit shape
- tiling pattern

Discover

A compound shape is made up of two or more simple shapes, such as triangles, squares, circles and rectangles. An example is a hexagon placed on top of a square.

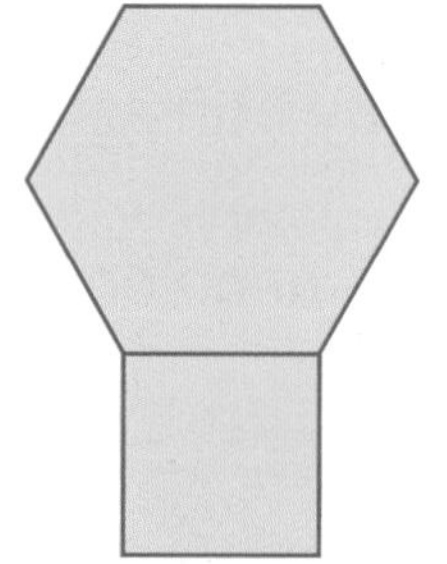

Learn

Tiling patterns can be created by translating compound shapes.

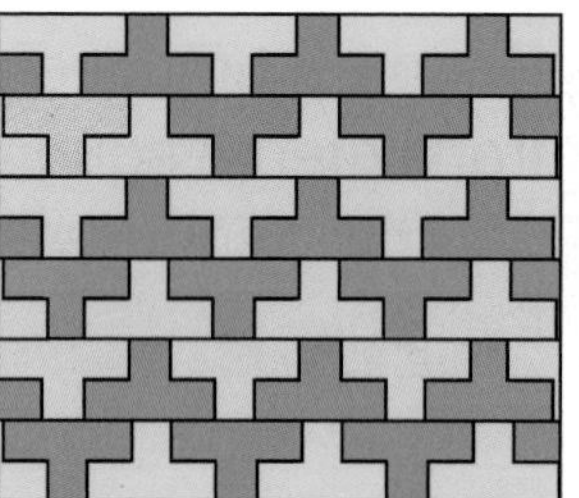
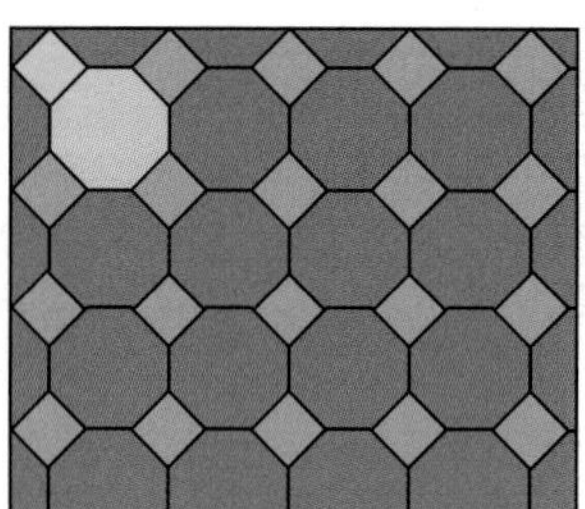
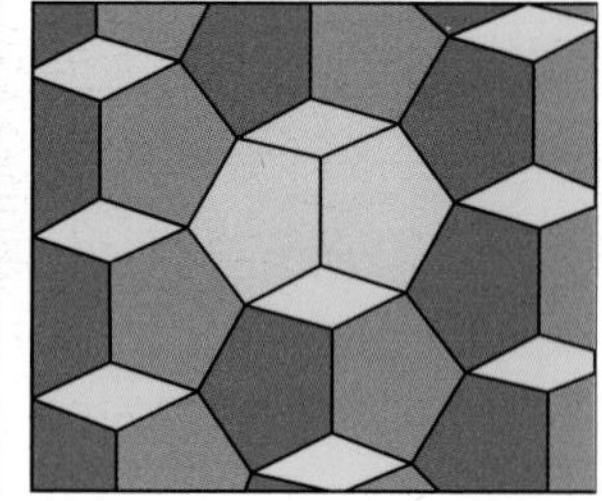

Example

The compound shape A, made from four squares, is translated three ways to make a tiling pattern. A set of interlocking L-shapes is made by translating either 1 square right and 1 square up, or 1 square left and 1 square down. Another is made by translating 1 square down, 3 squares right and repeating the translations at this point.

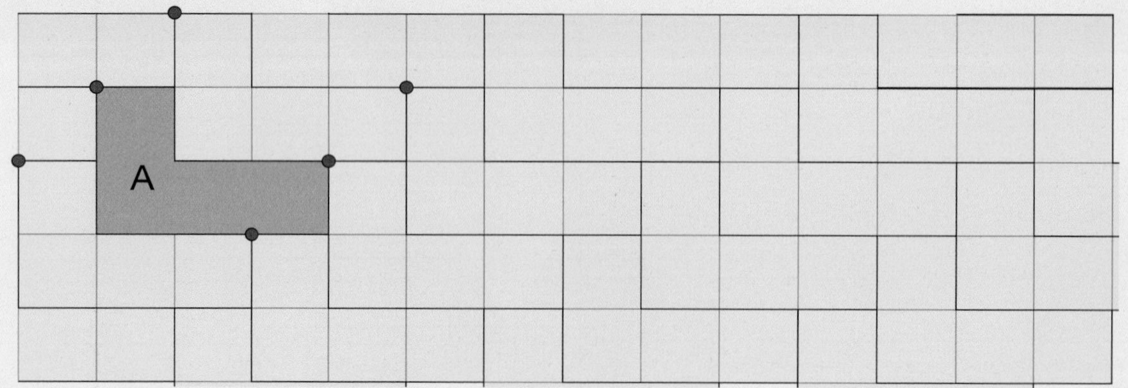

Geometry

Lesson 1: **Measuring length**

- Estimate and measure length or height using standard units (m, cm, mm)

Key words

- millimetre (mm)
- centimetre (cm)
- metre (m)
- kilometre (km)
- scale
- zero mark

Discover

You need to measure the length and height of objects to describe their size. This is important when you want to change something that has a fixed size and shape.

Learn

You measure length in millimetres (mm), centimetres (cm), metres (m) and kilometres (km). For greater accuracy, measure in millimetres or centimetres. For longer lengths, use metres or kilometres.

1 millimetre is about …

1 centimetre is about …

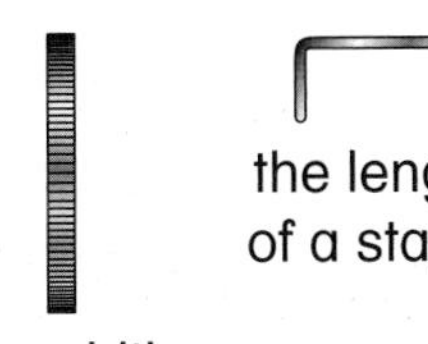

the width of a coin

the length of a staple

1 metre is about …

the width of a door

1 kilometre is about …

how far you can walk in 15 minutes

To use a ruler, line up one end of an object with the zero mark. Read the measurement at the other end of the object.

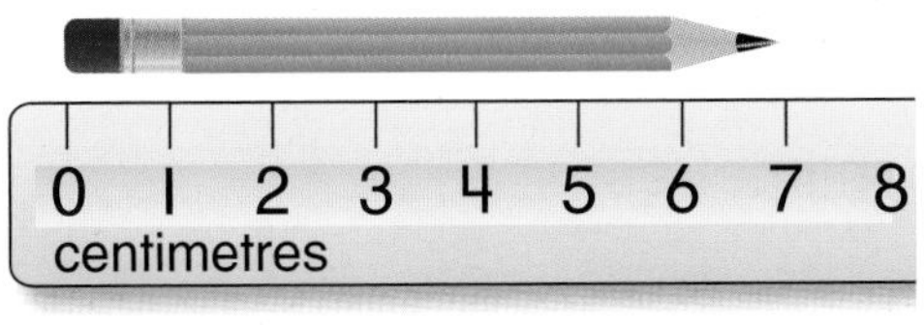

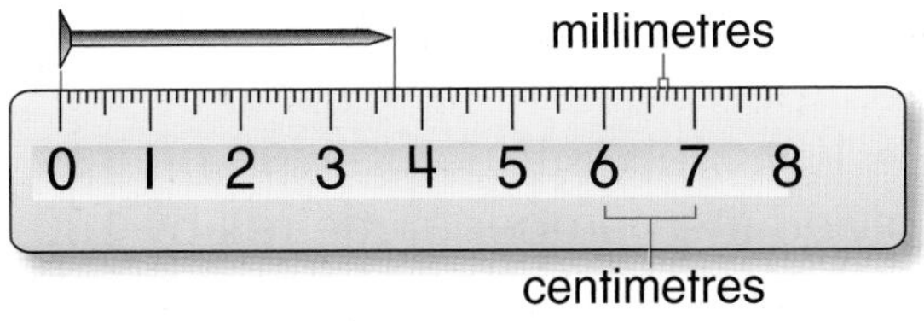

Example

This flute is 61 centimetres in length.

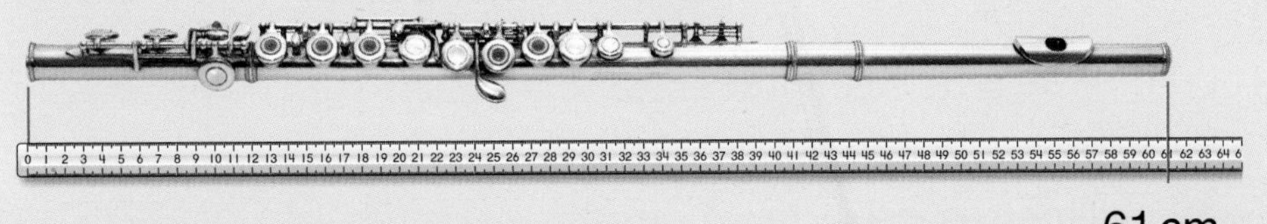

Lesson 2: **Converting units**

- Know the relationships between kilometres, metres, centimetres and millimetres
- Use multiplication to convert from larger to smaller units of length

Key words
- **millimetre (mm)**
- **centimetre (cm)**
- **metre (m)**
- **kilometre (km)**
- **place value**
- **metric unit**

Discover

Sometimes you need to convert between different units of length, particularly if you want a unit to suit your situation.

You may want to know the length of a running course in metres instead of kilometres, or the width of a piece of wood in millimetres instead of centimetres.

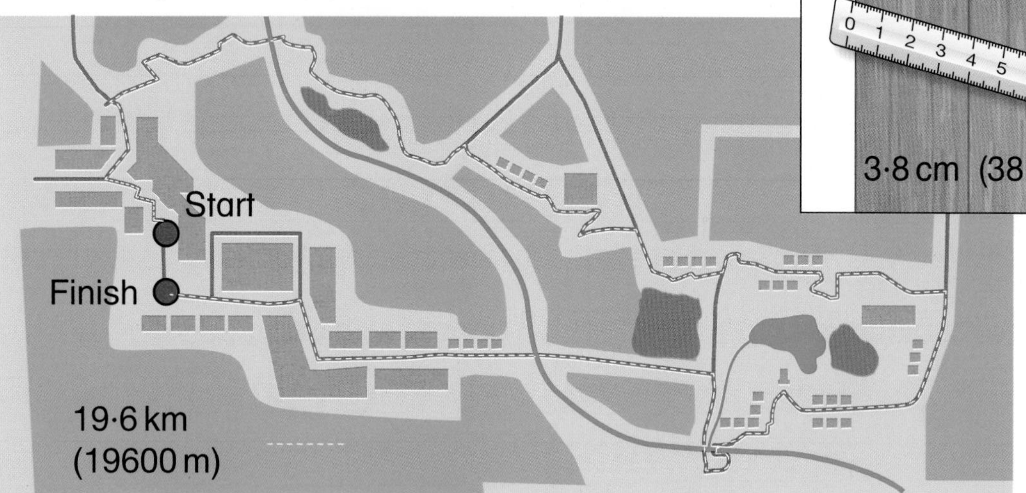

Learn

1 km = 1000 m. Convert kilometres to metres by multiplying the number of metres by 1000.

1 metre = 100 centimetres. Convert metres to centimetres by multiplying the number of metres by 100.

1 centimetre = 10 millimetres. Convert centimetres to millimetres by multiplying the number of centimetres by 10.

Example

3·7 km = 3·7 × 1000 metres = 3700 metres

8·3 m = 8·3 × 100 centimetres = 830 centimetres

97·1 cm = 97·1 × 10 millimetres = 971 millimetres

Lesson 3: **Ordering and rounding length**

- Order measurements in mixed units
- Round units to the nearest whole unit

Key words
- millimetre (mm)
- centimetre (cm)
- metre (m)
- kilometre (km)
- round
- place value

Discover

Rounding makes numbers easier to work with. For example, if you ask someone to clip off 1 m from a hedge that is 2 m 98 cm high, you might round the original measurement to 3 m.

Learn

When rounding to the nearest whole number, you round the units digit. Focus on the tenths digit:

- If it's less than 5, round the number down by removing the decimal part of the number.
- If it's 5 or more, round the number up by adding 1 to the units digit and removing the decimal fraction.

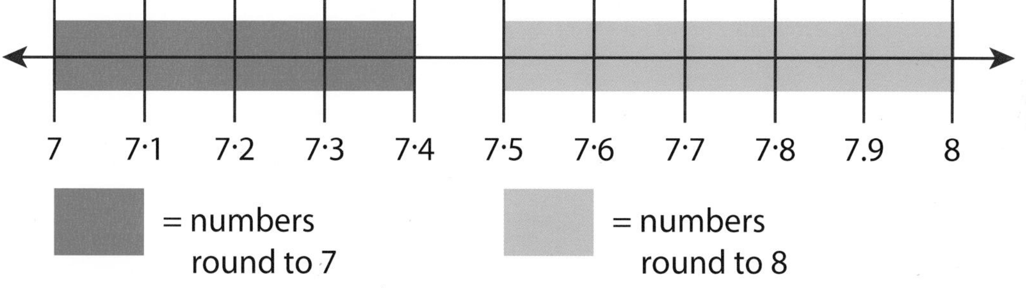

To order mixed units of length, convert the measurements to a common unit.

Example

48·5 m rounds to 49 m

90·1 cm rounds to 90 cm

To order the lengths 235 cm, 4·73 m and 4500 mm:

235 cm = 2·35 m (235 ÷ 100)

4500 mm = 4·5 m (4500 ÷ 1000)

The correct order is 235 cm (2·35 m), 4500 mm (4·5 m), 4·73 m

Lesson 4: **Measuring lines**

- Draw lines to a required length (cm or mm)
- Measure lines to the nearest centimetre or millimetre

Key words
- millimetre (mm)
- centimetre (cm)
- zero mark

Discover

The rulers are marked with red lines. What measurement does each line represent?

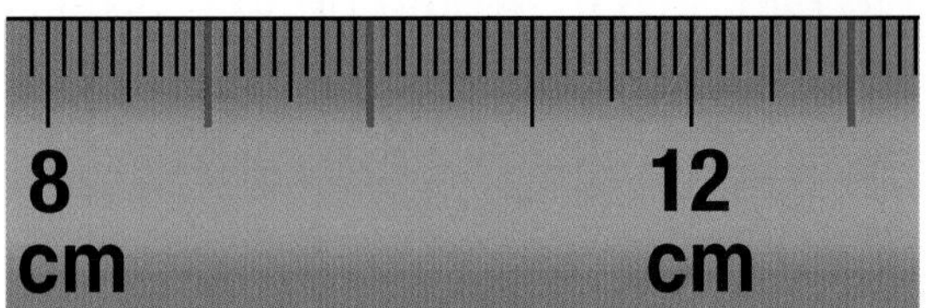

Learn

You can use a ruler to measure an object to the nearest millimetre, then round to the nearest centimetre.

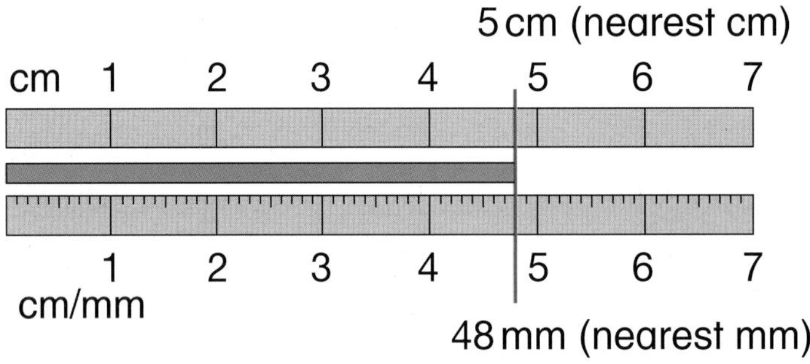

Example

The length of the crayon is somewhere between 41 and 42 mm. On close examination the end of the crayon is closer to 41 mm. Round to the nearest centimetre – this is 4 cm.

The length of the pencil is 5 cm and 4 mm, or 5 cm if rounded to the nearest centimetre.

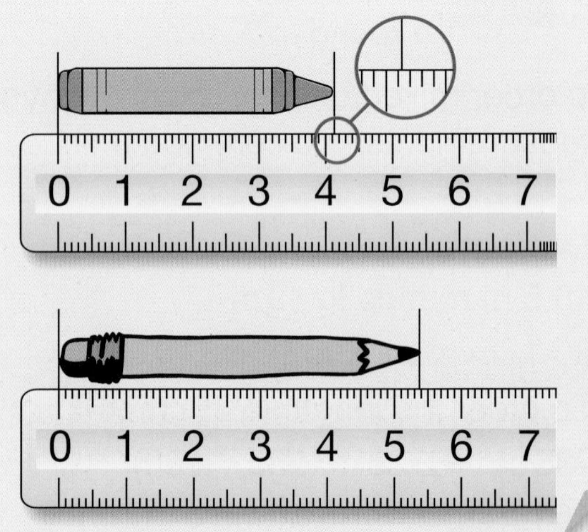

Measure

Lesson 1: **Measuring mass**

- Estimate and measure mass using standard units (g, kg)

Key words
- mass
- kilogram (kg)
- gram (g)
- scale
- division

Discover

It is important to be able to measure mass accurately. Businesses measure packages to calculate delivery costs; companies sending goods by air, ship or rail measure cargo to prevent overloading vehicles; and farmers weigh their livestock to know how much to feed them.

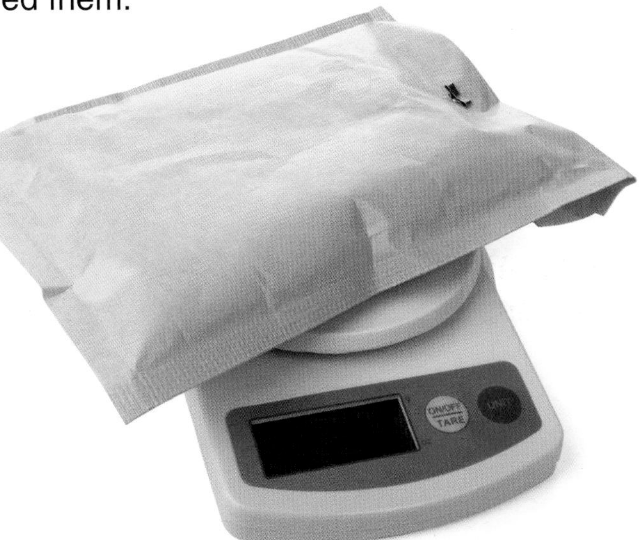

Learn

You measure mass in kilograms (kg) and grams (g). For greater accuracy, you measure in grams. A gram is about the mass of a paperclip. For larger masses, you measure in kilograms. A kilogram is about the mass of 1 litre of water.

Example

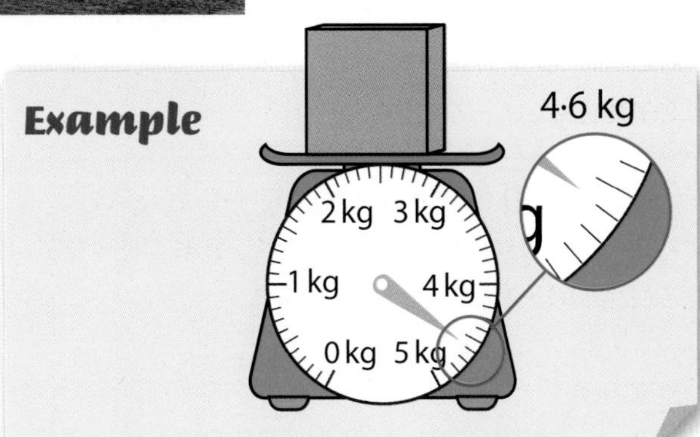

Workbook page 196

Lesson 2: **Converting units**

- Know the relationship between kilograms and grams
- Use multiplication to convert from larger to smaller units of mass

Key words
- **mass**
- **kilogram (kg)**
- **gram (g)**
- **place value**

Discover

Sometimes you need to convert between different units of mass, particularly if you want a unit to suit your situation.

You may want to know the mass of some flour or pasta in grams instead of kilograms.

Learn

1 kg = 1000 g

Convert kilograms to grams by multiplying the number of kilograms by 1000.

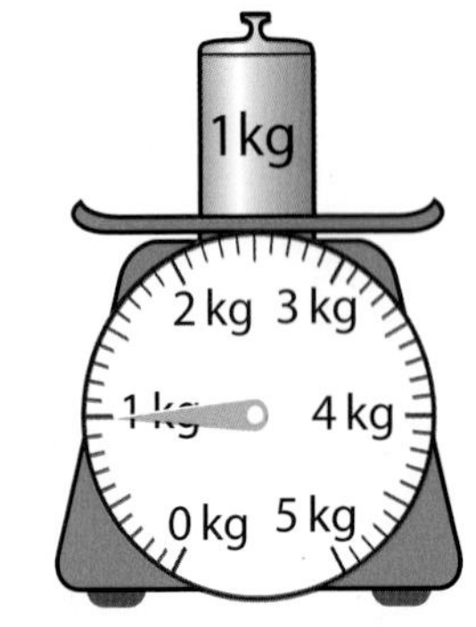

1 kilogram = 1000 grams

Example

1 kg = 1000 g

← Digits move 3 places to the left

2·100 kg → 2100 g

Lesson 3: **Ordering and rounding mass**

- Order mass measurements in mixed units
- Round numbers on scales to the nearest kilogram and to the nearest 100 g

Key words

- mass
- gram (g)
- kilogram (kg)
- round
- decimal place

Discover

When baggage is loaded onto an aircraft, the heaviest items are usually placed in the central cargo area, with the lighter items at the front and back.

If cargo was placed on board without comparing and ordering the mass of individual items, it would result in an unstable aircraft.

Learn

To order mass measurements in mixed units, you need to convert them into the same unit.

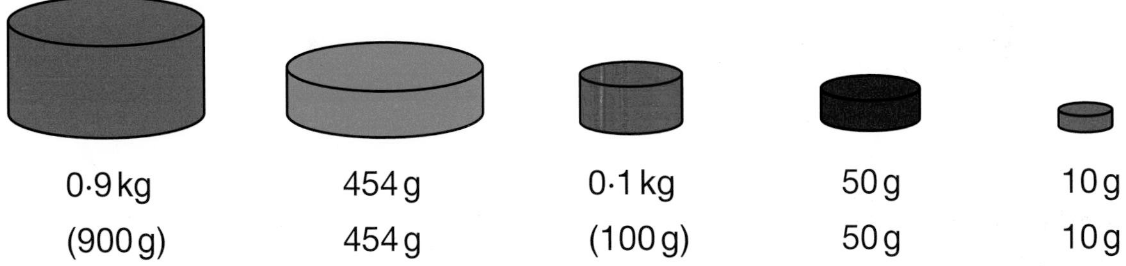

0·9 kg	454 g	0·1 kg	50 g	10 g
(900 g)	454 g	(100 g)	50 g	10 g

0·9 kg can be rounded to the nearest kilogram: 1 kg.

454 g can be rounded to the nearest 100 g: 500 g.

Example

Put these masses in order: 3479 g, 3·7 kg, 2345 g, 2·4 kg

Order by converting them to the same unit:
2345 g, 2·4 kg (2400 g), 3479 g, 3·7 kg (3700 g)

Round to the nearest kg: 2·4 kg = 2 kg   3·7 kg = 4 kg

Round to the nearest 100 g: 2345 g = 2300 g   3479 g = 3500 g

Workbook page 200

Lesson 4: **Reading weighing scales**

- Know the equivalent of $\frac{1}{2}$, $\frac{1}{4}$, and $\frac{1}{10}$ of a kilogram in grams
- Find the value of each interval on a scale to give an approximate reading of mass
- Use different scales to measure the same object

Key words
- **kilogram (kg)**
- **mass**
- **gram (g)**
- **scale**
- **division**

Discover

Reading measurements accurately is important in subjects such as science, as well as at home.

Learn

$\frac{1}{4}$kg = 250 g $\frac{1}{2}$kg = 500 g $\frac{1}{10}$kg = 100 g

Knowing the value of each scale division allows you to read scales accurately.

For the first two scales, each division marks 250 g; for the scale on the right, each division marks 10 g.

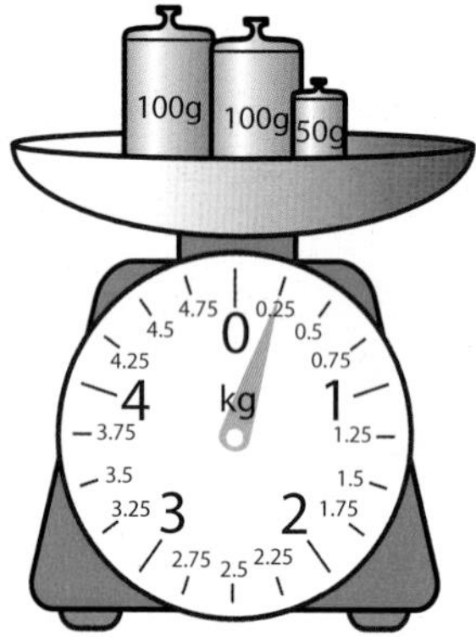

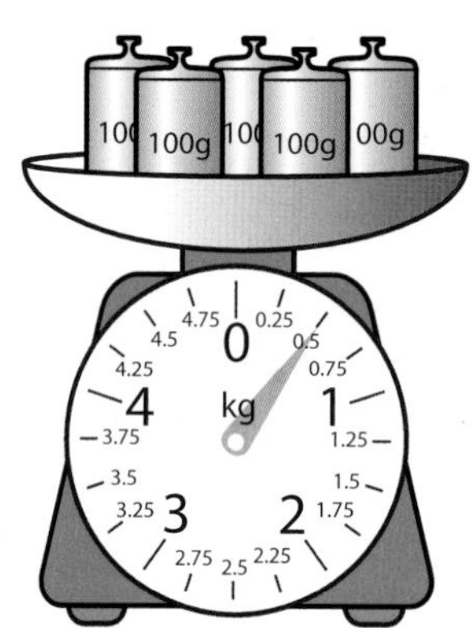

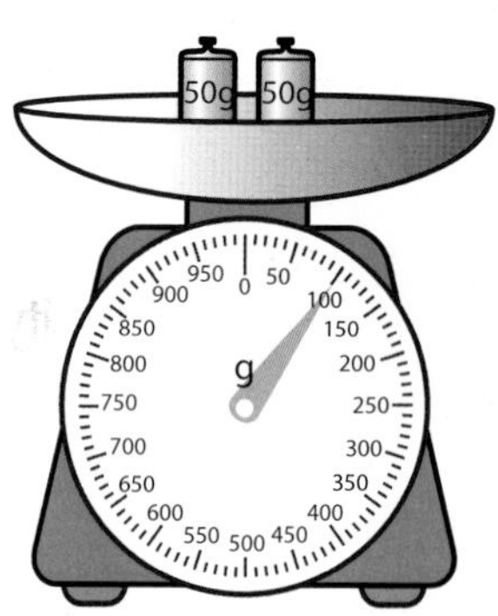

Example

Calculating difference

Scale A: divisions of 0·25 kg

Reading: 1·25 kg (or 1250 g)

Scale B: divisions of 10 g

Reading: 360 g

Difference: 1250 g – 360 g = 890 g

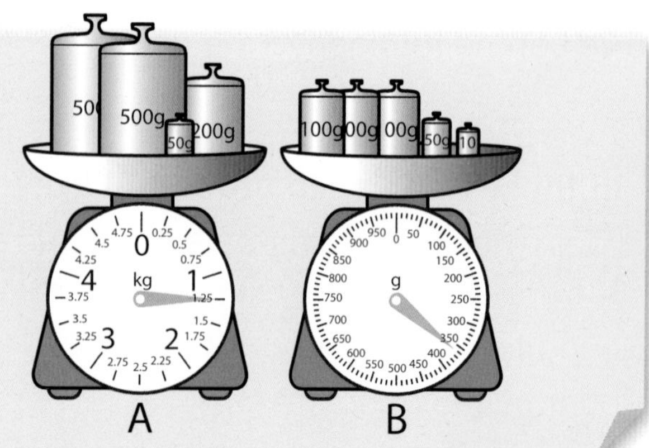

Lesson 1: **Measuring capacity**

- Estimate and measure capacity using standard units (ml, *l*)

Key words
- capacity
- litre (*l*)
- millilitre (ml)
- scale
- division

Discover

It is important to measure capacity accurately.
When making a milkshake, you need to know that the blender will hold all the ingredients. When driving a long distance, a driver needs to know the fuel tank contains enough petrol for the journey.

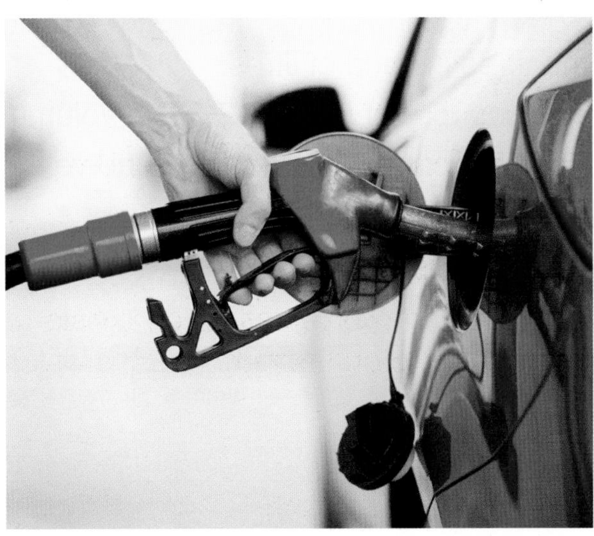

Learn

You measure capacity in litres (*l*) and millilitres (ml). For greater accuracy, you measure in millilitres. A millilitre is about 20 drops of water. For larger capacities, you measure in litres. A litre is about four cups of water.

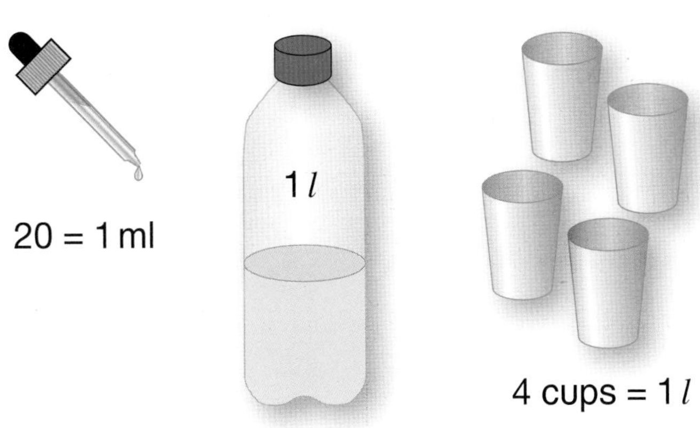

Example

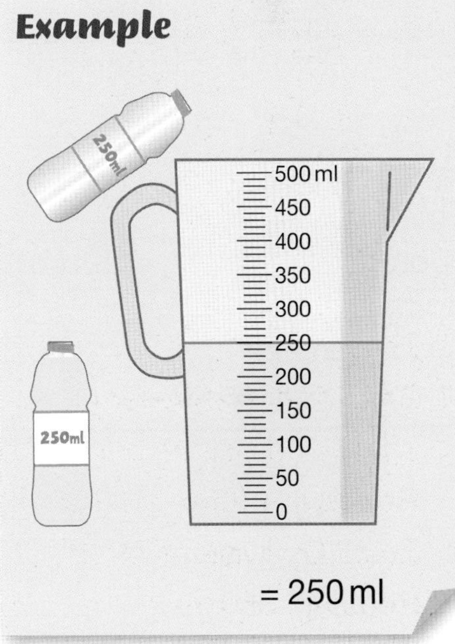

= 250 ml

Workbook page 204

Lesson 2: **Converting units**

- Know the relationship between litres and millilitres
- Use multiplication to convert from larger to smaller units of capacity

Key words
- capacity
- litre (l)
- millilitre (ml)
- place value

Discover

Sometimes you need to convert between different units of capacity, particularly if you want a unit to suit your situation.

You may want to know the volume of liquid in a bottle or flask in millilitres instead of litres.

The capacity of jug A is 2 l. The volume of water is 1200 ml.

The capacity of jug B is 1·5 l. The volume of water is 1100 ml.

A 2 l

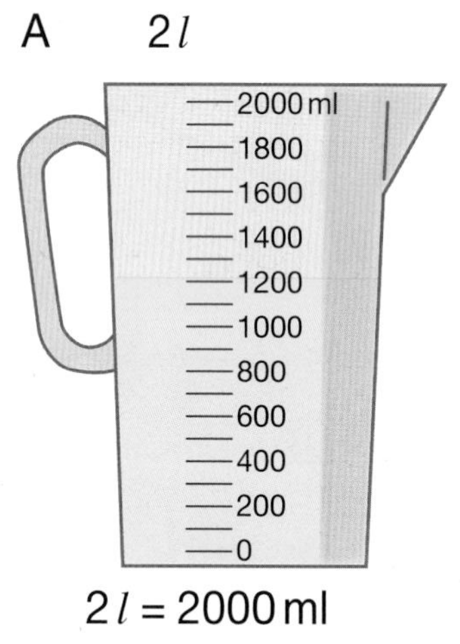

2 l = 2000 ml

B 1·5 l

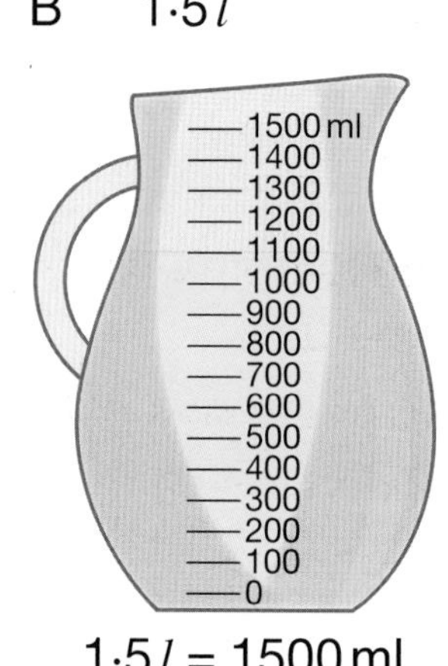

1·5 l = 1500 ml

Learn

1 l = 1000 ml

Convert litres to millilitres by multiplying the number of litres by 1000.

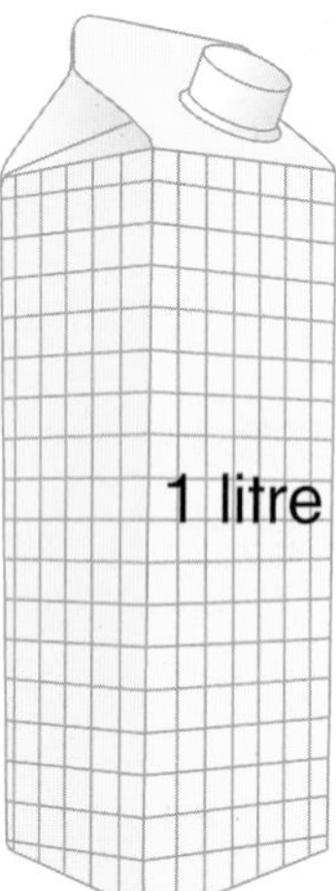

1 litre = 1000 ml

Example

This container has a capacity of 10 l. The volume of water is 3·7 l.

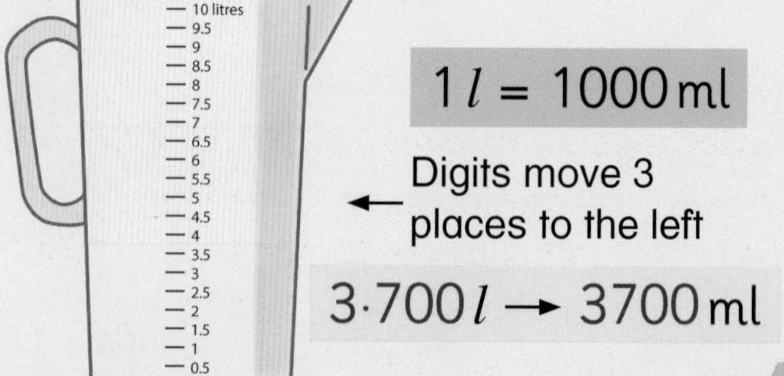

1 l = 1000 ml

Digits move 3 places to the left

3·700 l → 3700 ml

Lesson 3: **Ordering and rounding capacity**

- Order capacity measurements in mixed units
- Round numbers on scales to the nearest litre and to the nearest 100 ml

Key words
- capacity
- millilitre (ml)
- litre (*l*)
- round
- decimal place

Discover

You can place containers in order of capacity, even if the measurements are given in mixed units.

890 ml

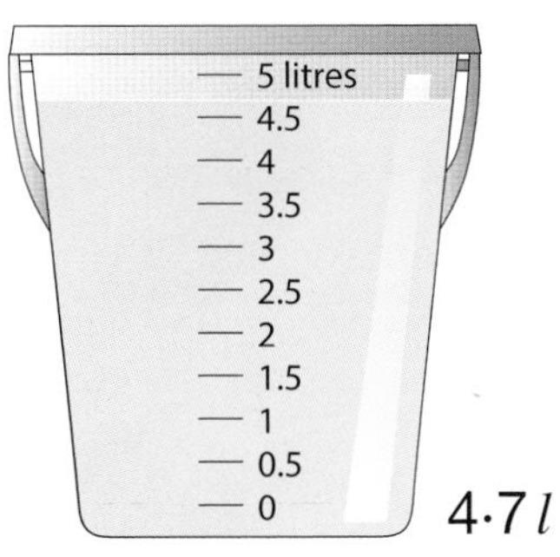

4·7 *l*

2 *l* 300 ml

Learn

To order capacity measurements in mixed units, you need to convert to the same unit.

0·7 *l* can be rounded to the nearest litre: 1 *l*.

2339 ml can be rounded to the nearest 100 ml: 2300 ml.

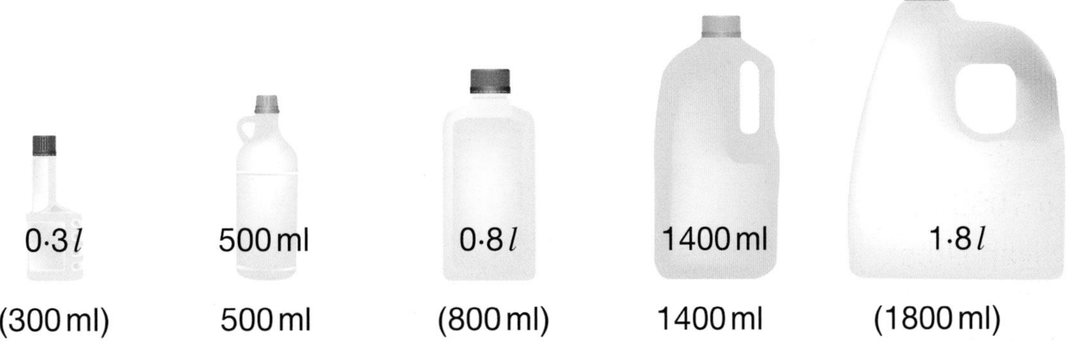

(300 ml) 500 ml (800 ml) 1400 ml (1800 ml)

Example

Order these capacities: 4650 ml, 4·6 *l*, 4605 ml, 4·4 *l*

Order by converting them to the same unit:

4·4 *l* (4400 ml), 4·6 *l* (4600 ml), 4605 ml, 4650 ml

Round to the nearest litre: 4·6 *l* = 5 *l* 4·4 *l* = 4 *l*

Round to the nearest 100 ml: 4650 ml = 4700 g 4605 ml = 4600 g

Measure

Lesson 4: **Reading capacity scales**

Key words
- capacity
- millilitre (ml)
- litre (l)
- scale
- division

- Know the equivalent of $\frac{1}{2}$, $\frac{1}{4}$, and $\frac{1}{10}$ of a litre in millilitres
- Find the value of each interval on a scale to give an approximate reading of capacity
- Use different scales to measure the same container

Discover

It is important to read scales accurately to ensure the correct amount has been measured. For example, if you need to take medicine, you must take the right amount. Too little might not work; too much could be dangerous.

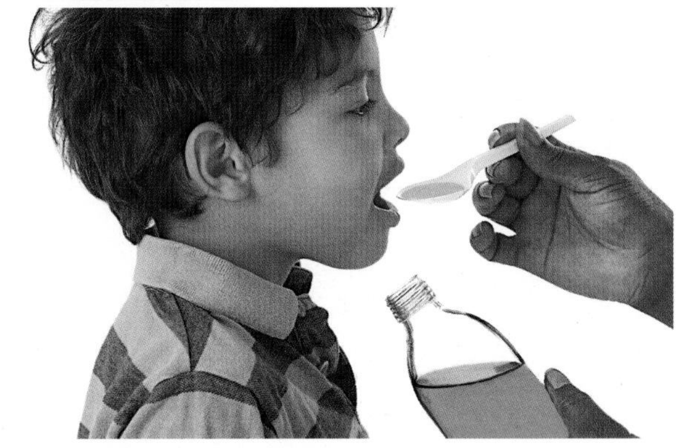

Learn

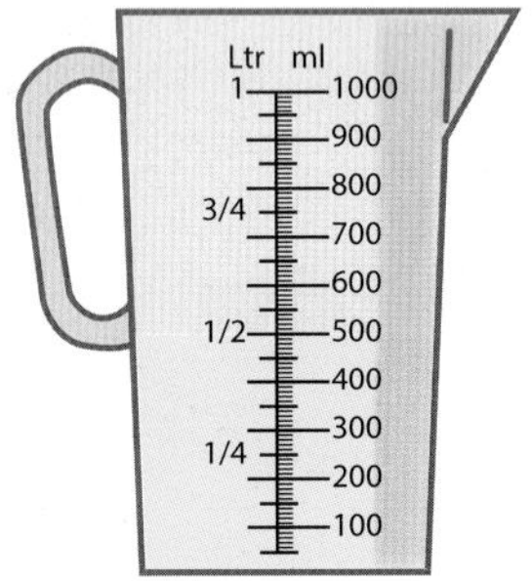

$\frac{1}{2}l = 500\,\text{ml}$

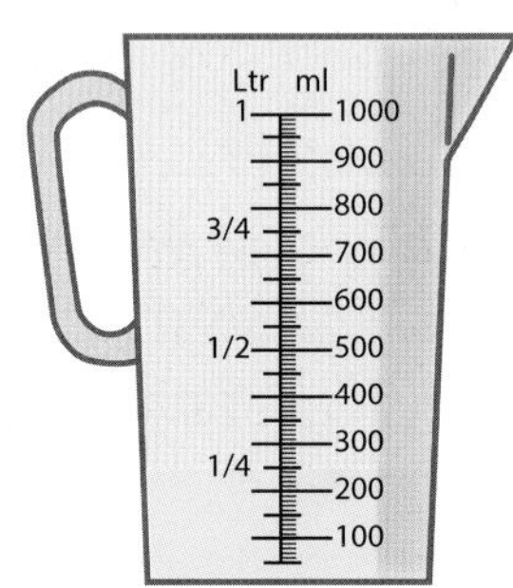

$\frac{1}{4}l = 250\,\text{ml}$

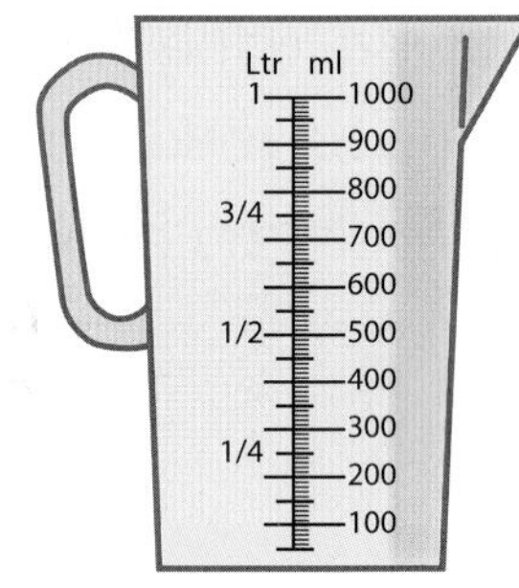

$\frac{1}{10}l = 100\,\text{ml}$

Knowing the value of each scale division allows you to read scales accurately.
Each division on the right of the scale is 100 ml. Each division on the left is $\frac{1}{4}l$.

Example

Reading between the divisions

The level is between 80 ml and 90 ml but, looking carefully at eye level, you can see it is closer to 80 ml.

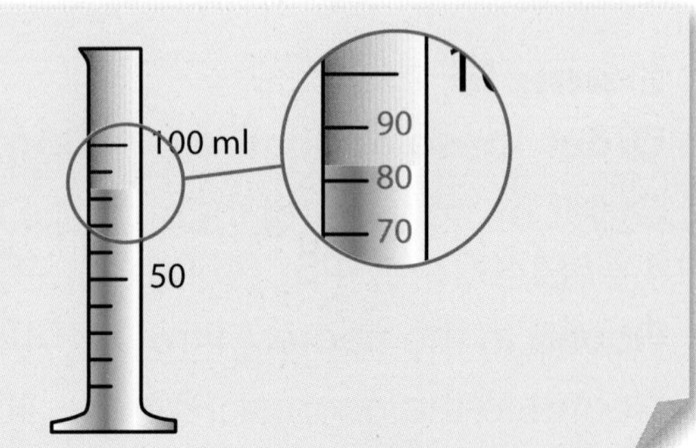

Measure

Lesson 1: **Interpreting graphs and tables**

- Draw and read data from frequency tables, pictograms and bar line charts

Key words
- tally chart
- frequency table
- pictogram
- bar line chart

Discover

Organising information in tables and graphs makes it easier and quicker to interpret.

It is important to know how to create and interpret tables and graphs. They play a crucial role in many areas, from scientific research to weather forecasts.

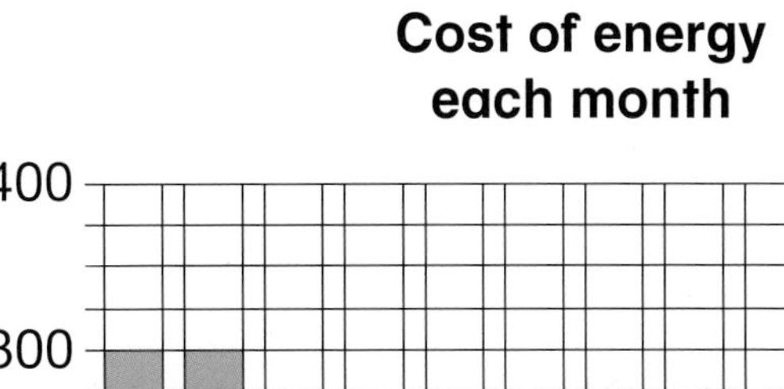

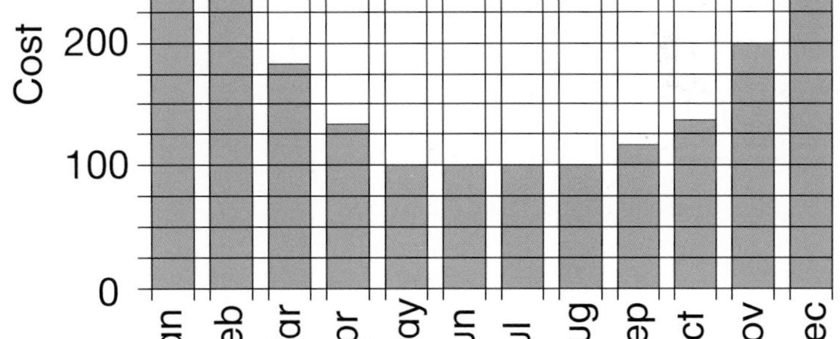

Learn

A bar line chart is similar to a bar chart, but with lines. It represents data that can only take certain numbers (like whole numbers) or categories. Remember:

- length of bar represents frequency
- do not join tops of bars.

Example

This graph shows:

- Most people have brown eyes.
- Blue is the least common eye colour.
- 4 more people have hazel eyes than blue eyes.

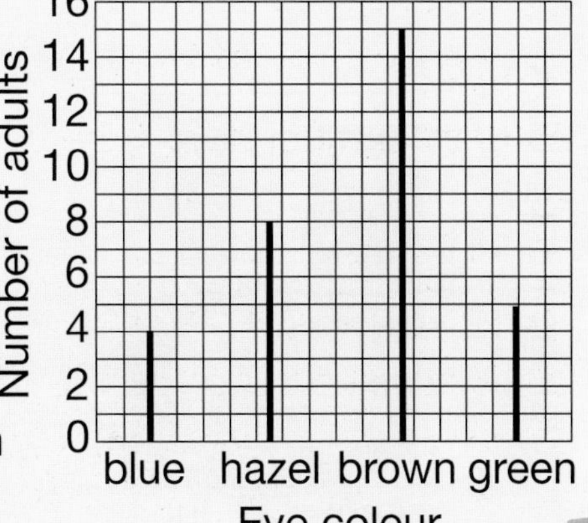

Lesson 2: **Changing the scale**

- Read and interpret data for tables and graphs where the vertical axis is labelled in intervals greater than 1

Key words
- tally chart
- frequency table
- pictogram
- bar line chart
- scale
- interval

Discover

The 'look' of a graph can be changed quite dramatically by adjusting the scale on the vertical axis, although the data it is presenting is actually unchanged.

For example, the scale can be altered to make bar heights seem more dramatic, or less significant.

Choosing an appropriate scale is more important than simply making the graph fit on the paper.

Car sales (graph 1)

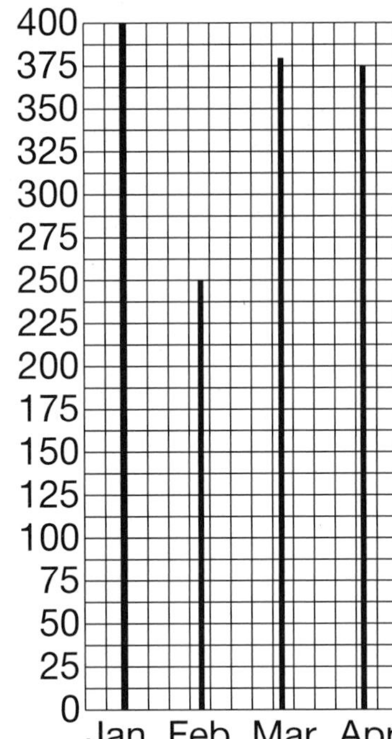

Car sales (graph 2)

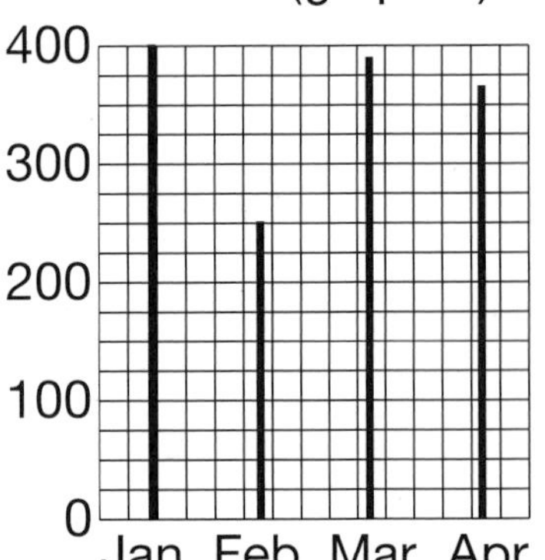

Learn

A graph can be altered by changing its scale. The data in two graphs may be identical, but changing the scale of the vertical axis can change how big the differences look to a reader.

Example

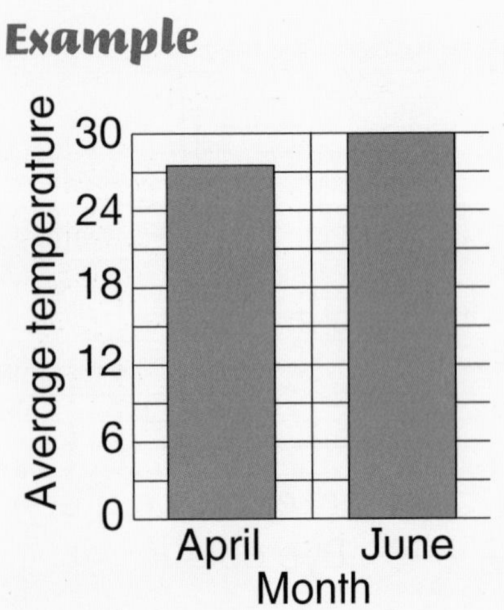

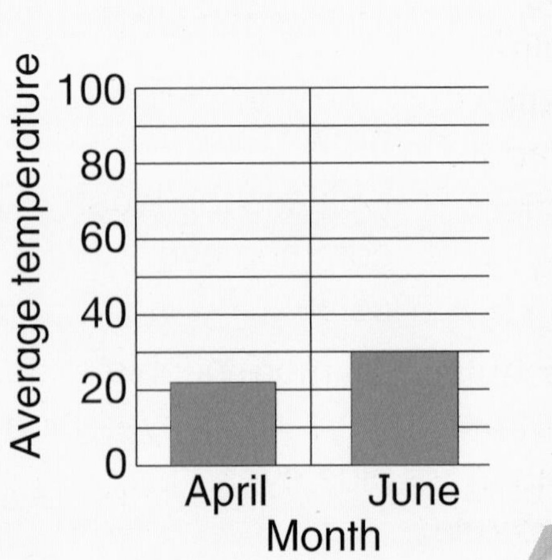

Handling data

Lesson 3: **Line graphs**

- Construct and interpret a simple line graph

Key words
- horizontal axis
- vertical axis
- line graph
- scale

Discover

A line graph shows how something changes over time, for example, how the temperature changes over days, months or years. Line graphs are useful in scientific research, weather monitoring and other situations where a change in the quantity of something needs to be studied.

Temperature change

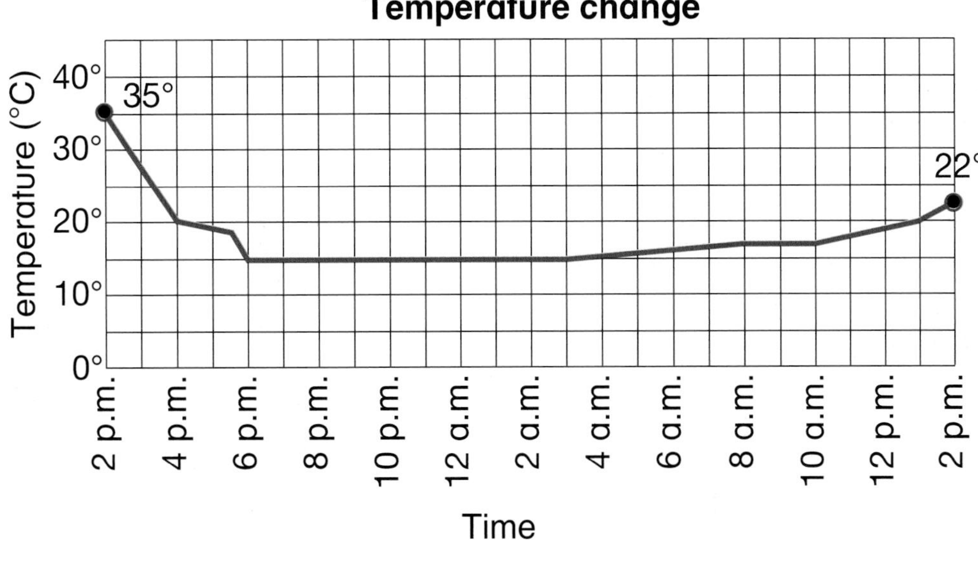

Learn

Line graphs are commonly used for measurements made at regular time intervals, for example, daily, weekly or monthly. The quantity measured is recorded on the vertical axis, with time along the horizontal axis. It is important to choose a suitable scale, to plot points accurately and to join them up using a pencil and ruler.

Example

Number of laptops sold from January to June

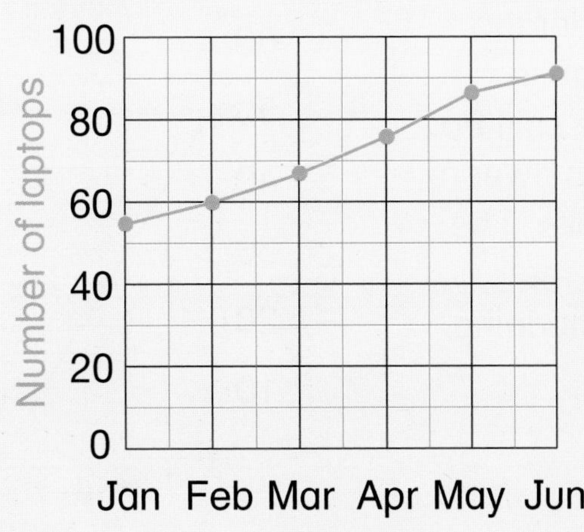

Lesson 4: **Intermediate points**

- Interpret line graphs and decide whether intermediate points have meaning

Key words
- discrete data
- continuous data
- intermediate point

Discover

We use different types of graph to represent different types of data. What other types of data would be best plotted on Graph A? And Graph B?

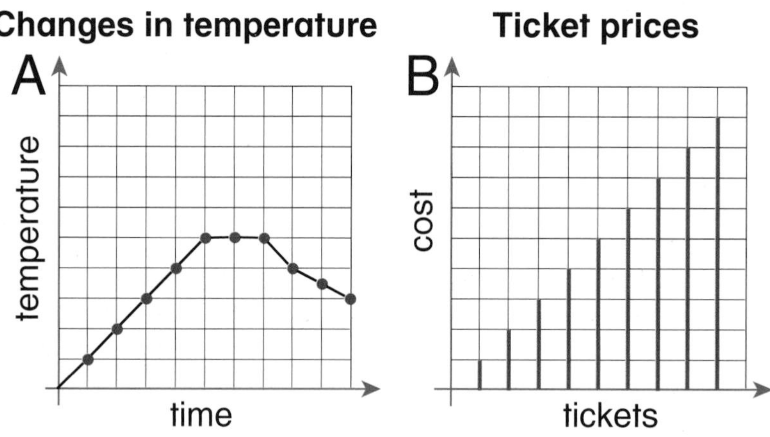

Learn and Example

Some data is continuous and can take on any value. Consider the fuel level for a car on a journey. The level can be any value between full and empty. The intermediate points between the plotted points have meaning.

Other data is discrete – it can only be certain numbers. Consider the cost of buying books. Books cannot be split up; there is no data between, say, 1 and 2 books. The spaces between the points have no meaning.

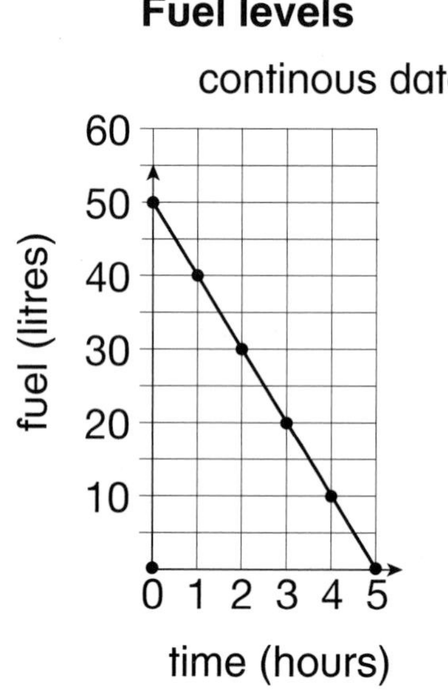

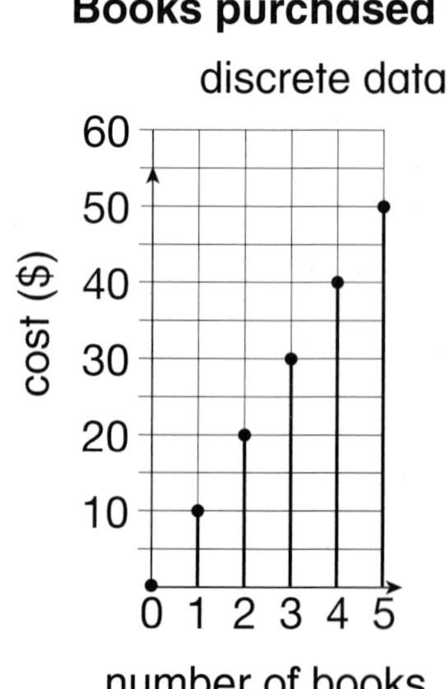

Lesson 5: **Mode**

- Find and interpret the mode of a set of data

Key words
- set
- mode

Discover

The mode of a set of data is the item or value that occurs most often. Think about book publishing – why do you think it is important to know the most popular book? In shoe manufacture, why do you think it is essential to know the most popular shoe size?

Learn

To find the mode of a set of items – the item that appears in the set the most – it helps to list the numbers in numerical order. Count the frequency of each number and identify the value that appears most.

18, 21, 11, 21, 15, 19, 17, 21, 17

11, 15, 17, 17, 18, 19, (21, 21, 21) MODE

11 - 1   18-1

15-1   19-1

17-2   21-3

Example

Goals scored per match: 3, 4, 3, 1, 0, 2, 3, 2

Order: 0, 1, 2, 2, (3, 3, 3), 4

most frequent

Mode: 3

Lesson 6: **Collecting data**

- To test a hypothesis by collecting and organising data from an enquiry

Key words
- data
- hypothesis
- collect

Discover

Asking questions about how the world around you works is an important part of maths, science and many other subjects. Mathematicians and scientists begin with a hypothesis – an idea for something that might be true, but is not yet tested – and set about finding evidence to support it.

Average daily visitors to a shop

Number of people: 0, 10, 20, 30, 40, 50, 60, 70, 80, 90, 100

Time: 8 a.m., 9 a.m., 10 a.m., 11 a.m., 12 p.m., 1 p.m., 2 p.m., 3 p.m.

I think the busiest time of day is 1 p.m.

Learn

We can think of a hypothesis as a 'big question' that needs answering.

Testing a hypothesis means asking, and answering, other questions:

- How can we find out if this is true?
- What information shall we collect?
- How shall we organise it?

Answers to these questions help us decide which data to collect and how.

I made a tally of visitors for each time period. Then I found the frequency.

Example

Time	Tally	Frequency
8 a.m.	卌 卌 II	12
9 a.m.	卌 卌 卌 卌 III	23
10 a.m.	卌 卌 卌 卌 卌 IIII	29
11 a.m.	卌 卌 卌 卌 卌 卌 卌 II	37
12 p.m.	卌 卌 卌 卌 卌 卌 卌 卌 卌 III	48
1 p.m.	卌 卌 卌 卌 卌 卌 卌 卌 卌 卌 卌 卌 卌 卌 卌 卌 卌 IIII	89
2 p.m.	卌 卌 卌 卌 卌 卌 卌 卌 卌 卌 卌 卌 卌 II	67
3 p.m.	卌 卌 卌 卌 卌 卌 卌 卌 卌 卌 I	51

Lesson 7: Presenting data

- To test a hypothesis by presenting data from an enquiry and drawing conclusions

Key words
- data
- hypothesis
- conclusion

Discover

It is important to represent the results of an enquiry as clearly as possible, to make it easier to interpret results and draw conclusions. This means choosing the right type of graph and deciding on the most appropriate scale.

score	frequency (f)
1	4
2	9
3	6
4	7
5	3
6	2

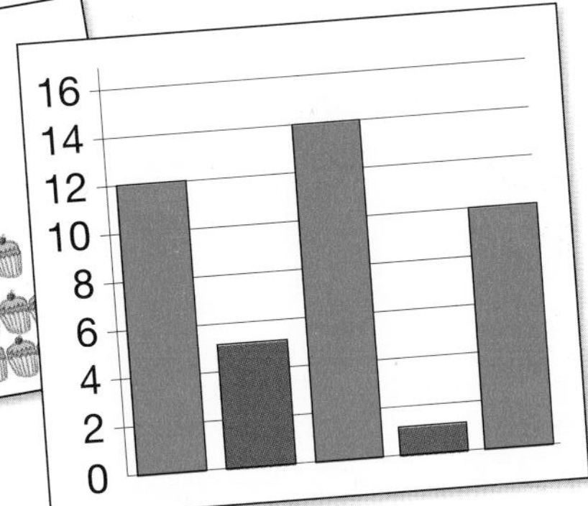

Learn

When deciding how best to represent data, it's good to think about the end goal – what do you want the reader to focus on? Do you want to show a trend over time, or show values by category?

Line graphs work best for continuous data, whereas bar charts, bar line charts and pictograms work best for discrete data.

Example

Yes, the graph supports my prediction that 1 p.m. is the busiest time of the day!

Lesson 8: **Probability**

- Describe the likelihood of an event happening using the language of chance

Key words
- likelihood
- chance
- impossible
- certain
- even chance

Discover

Probability is the study of random events – how likely something is to happen. Understanding probability is essential for appreciating games of chance and weather forecasts.

MON	TUE	WED	THU	FRI	SAT	SUN
40%	40%	60%	40%	40%	30%	50%

Learn

Probability can be shown on a probability scale.

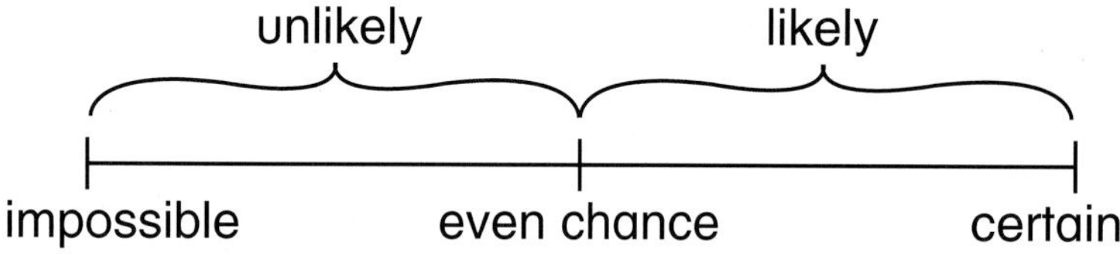

We use the terms 'certain', 'likely', 'even chance', 'unlikely' and 'impossible' to describe how likely an event is to happen.

Example

Impossible to spin '5'
Even chance of spinning '1' or '2'.

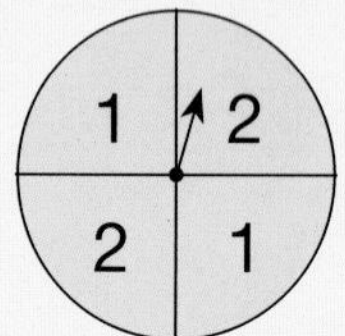

Certain a '1' will be spun.

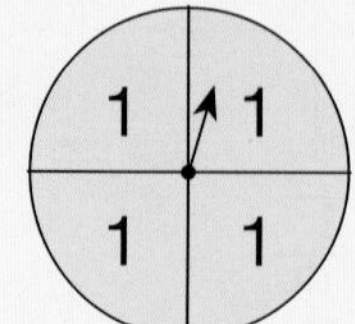

Likely a '1' will be spun but **unlikely** a '2' will be spun.

Notes

Notes

Notes

Photo acknowledgements

Every effort has been made to trace copyright holders.

Any omission will be rectified at the first opportunity.

Front cover and title page sylv1rob1/Shutterstock, p2 Sura Nualpradid/Shutterstock, p3 Billion Photos/ Shutterstock, p6 Marcos Mesa Sam Wordley/ Shutterstock, p7 Tristan3D/Shutterstock, p11 Gts/ Shutterstock, p17 ImagePixel/Shutterstock, p18 Max Sudakov/Shutterstock, p19 rmnoa357/Shutterstock, p20tl studiovin/Shutterstock, p20tr WilleeCole Photography/Shutterstock, p20bl Africa Studio/ Shutterstock, p20br Gnilenkov Aleksey/Shutterstock, p24 Oleksiy Mark/Shutterstock, p33 Maximilian Laschon/Shutterstock, p35l RTimages/Shutterstock, p35tr america365/Shutterstock, p35br america365/ Shutterstock, p39 iDraw/iStockphoto, p40 inzpires/ Shutterstock, p41 artisticco/Thinkstock, p44 Matthew Cole/Shutterstock, p52t majeczka/Shutterstock, p52c Dhoxax/Shutterstock, p52b majeczka/Shutterstock, p53 Pavel L Photo and Video/Shutterstock, p55 Tribalium/Shutterstock, p56 (dollars) Rashevskyi Viacheslav/Shutterstock, p56 (people) RealVector/ Shutterstock, p58 Lindsay Helms/Shutterstock, p59 Joseph Sohm/Shutterstock, p64 Kutlayev Dmitry/ Shutterstock, p65 Slavoljub Pantelic/Shutterstock, p66 Tribalium/Shutterstock, p68 nimon/Shutterstock, p70 Linda Vostrovska/Shutterstock, p71 KoQ Creative/Shutterstock, p73l Anilah/Shutterstock, p73c rSnapshotPhotos/Shutterstock, p73r Sharaieu/ Shutterstock, p74l Studio Barcelona/Shutterstock, p74cl lkpro/Shutterstock, p74cr RuthChoi/Shutterstock, p74cr homydesign/Shutterstock, p75l drpnncpptak/ Shutterstock, p75tr Franck Boston/Shutterstock, p75br ManuKro/Shutterstock, p76tl PRILL/Shutterstock, p76tr stockelements/Shutterstock, p76bl Nomad_Soul/ Shutterstock, p76br Kitch Bain/Shutterstock, p79tl Tupungato/Shutterstock, p79tr Photology1971/ Shutterstock, p79bl Sergio Bertino/Shutterstock, p79br horiyan/Shutterstock, p80bl hamdan/Shutterstock, p80bc vector work/Shutterstock, p80br villorejo/ Shutterstock, p81bl Katstudio/Shutterstock, p81bc josefkubes/Shutterstock, p81br Sergey Kohl/ Shutterstock, p83bl karamysh/Shutterstock, p83br Dmitry Bruskov/Shutterstock, p87l BOONCHUAY PROMJIAM/Shutterstock, p87c Albisoima/ Shutterstock, p87r Janis Smits/Shutterstock, p88l Edelwipix/Shutterstock, p88c majeczka/Shutterstock, p88r Samot/Shutterstock, p90l Jirayos Bumrungjit/ Shutterstock, p90cl Elnur/Shutterstock, p90cr Susan Law Cain/Shutterstock, p90r Monkey Business Images/ Shutterstock, p93t Djem/Shutterstock, p93cr grynold/ Shutterstock, p93b (flute) furtseff/Shutterstock, p97tl Rights Managed Yavuz Sariyildiz/Shutterstock, p97tr alexandre17/Shutterstock, p97b Nickolay Khoroshkov/ Shutterstock, p98tl flashgun/Shutterstock, p98tr Giuvaclik/Shutterstock, p98br Viktar Malyshchyts/ Shutterstock, p99 bibiphoto/Shutterstock, p100tr flashgun/Shutterstock, p101tl marilyn barbone/ Shutterstock, p101tr Syda Productions/Shutterstock, p103 attaphong/Shutterstock, p104 JPC-PROD/ Shutterstock, p105tl Tupungato/Shutterstock, p105tr Benoit Daoust/Shutterstock, p106tl Sorbis/ Shutterstock, p106tr Claudio Divizia/Shutterstock, p106bl Claudio Divizia/Shutterstock, p106br MStasy/ Shutterstock, p109 Shi Yali /Shutterstock, p110l Alison Hancock/Shutterstock, p110r shooarts/Shutterstock, p111l wavebreakmedia/Shutterstock, p111r iofoto/ Shutterstock, p117l zefart/Shutterstock, p117r panpote/Shutterstock.